Spiritual and Moral Development in Schools

John West-Burnham and
Vanessa Huws Jones

network
continuum

Continuum International Publishing Group
Network Continuum
The Tower Building   80 Maiden Lane, Suite 704
11 York Road   New York, NY 10038
SE1 7NX

www.networkcontinuum.co.uk
www.continuumbooks.com

British Library Cataloguing-in-Publication Data
A catalogue record for this book is available from the British Library.

ISBN: 978-8553-9138-3 (paperback)

Typeset by Neil Hawkins, ndesignuk.co.uk

Printed and bound in Great Britain by Cromwell Press Ltd, Trowbridge, Wiltshire

Contents

Part 1

Principles

Introduction

Our purpose in writing this book is to provide a resource for teachers, school leaders and all those with an interest in education in schools. Our focus is the spiritual and moral development of children – an aspect of school life that, all agree, is fundamentally important but one that is all too easily marginalized given the pressures of curriculum coverage and the emphasis on assessment. It is also an area that many people find difficult to conceptualize, articulate and understand personally and professionally. This book seeks to help to develop that understanding and to help create a common professional language in schools.

We approach the topic from two perspectives. First, we stress the importance of spiritual and moral development as an essential component of any conceptualization of what it means to be an educated person. Second, we believe that schools have the potential to be even richer spiritual and moral communities as well as developing as learning communities; indeed we believe that effective models of learning are essential to spiritual and moral growth.

The education system in England has always recognized the importance of spiritual and moral development in education. However, this has almost always been interpreted in a religious way which, for many, can be restrictive and insular. This is not a book about religion or faith, its approach is essentially humanistic. We believe that the spiritual and moral are essential elements of what makes us human, in many ways these dimensions give us our uniqueness as human beings. There are multiple pathways into spiritual and moral understanding; all have validity according to historical and cultural norms.

We are hoping that this book will provide a non-dogmatic approach to the spiritual and moral growth of children, which readers can apply to their own particular needs and context. Part 1 is designed to provide a background to the key themes for teachers and school leaders – we hope that it will support and facilitate professional debate and dialogue. Part 2 offers information, discussion, resources and strategies to explore the key themes of spiritual and moral development in the primary school. Each topic is introduced with an outline and discussion of issues and themes, and this is supported by examples of approaches and activities that might be used in schools. These suggestions are designed around two broad principles: (1) spiritual and moral development is about learning to think; and (2) this requires the ability to engage in dialogue and social interaction. Part 3 is a personal case study and reflection by Vanessa Huws Jones of the development of a school as a spiritual and moral community, embodying and developing the key ideas of the book.

We are very grateful to Ingrid Bradbury, Noreen Buckingham and Laura Chapman who have provided feedback on the text to ensure that we have given appropriate recognition to the spiritual and moral development of children. We are also very grateful to Ingrid Bradbury for managing the production of this book.

John West-Burnham
Vanessa Huws Jones
January 2007

Childhood,
1 happiness and education

For the Dalai Lama there is no doubt about the relationship between education and happiness:

> What is the purpose of our life? Of course, I believe that it is happiness. Our culture, our education, our economy – all human activities – should be meant for that goal. Nothing else. However, although we often assume that certain activities will enable us to achieve this goal of happiness, in reality, we are often deceived by our own ignorance or shortsightedness … gnorance causes pain and suffering not only for ourselves but for others as well.

> Therefore, in order to eliminate ignorance, education, no doubt, becomes very important. But even as knowledge can be very helpful, I think a good heart, a warm heart, can expel this shortsightedness. (1999, page 85)

Csikszentmihalyi (1997) comes to a remarkably similar conclusion but from a very different perspective based on empirical research and cognitive science:

> Happiness is the prototype of the positive emotions. As many a thinker since Aristotle has said, everything we do is ultimately aimed at experiencing happiness. We don't really want wealth, or health, or fame as such – we want these things because we hope that they will make us happy. But happiness we seek not because it will get us something else, but for its own sake. (pages 18–19)

This chapter explores the relationship between our understanding of childhood, the nature of education and the extent to which they contribute to happiness. In particular we are looking to create an explicit framework to support the discussion in the following chapters. This book focuses on spirituality and moral education in the broadest sense, rather than how to implement a specific curriculum. We are working from the premise that education and schooling are distinct activities and not synonymous, and that schooling is a necessary but not sufficient component of education. Further to this is our belief that education, especially in the context of spiritual and moral development, is a product of a wide range of variables of which the school is only a minor part. Family and community life will have an enormous impact on this dimension of education, as will personal ability, aptitude and motivation.

This chapter therefore focuses on clarifying and illuminating the way in which we can best understand the relationship between childhood, happiness and education, and spiritual and moral development.

Understanding childhood

Our cultural understanding of childhood seems to be polarized between a romantic belief in the essential innocence of children and the need to preserve that innocence as long as possible, and the belief that children need to be controlled, disciplined and civilized. These diametrically opposed beliefs are replicated in many contexts; they are essentially optimistic and pessimistic views of human nature. Equally, according to Cunningham (2006):

> A history of childhood can easily become a history of what adults have done to children. Children become the victims or the beneficiaries of adult actions. But children can also be agents in the making of their lives and their world. (page 16)

A view which he subsequently develops:

> But there is one striking difference between childhood now and childhood as it has been lived for most of the last millennium that may be worth reflecting on. Children in the past have been assumed to have capabilities that we now rarely think that they have … So fixated are we on giving our children a long and happy childhood that we downplay their abilities and their resilience. To think of children as potential victims in need of protection is a very modern outlook, and it probably does no-one a service. (ibid., page 245)

A deeply pessimistic view of current society would see childhood as a fragile and vulnerable concept. It is easy to point to the manifestations of materialism, in particular the cynical marketing to children of consumer goods, the pressures of fashion (witness any primary school disco) and what some might see as premature exposure to sexuality and violence. At the same time, changes in the nature of the family, for example the increasing number of single-parent and stepfamilies point to a very different experience of childhood; this is not necessarily negative but different and diverse.

If childhood is seen as a transitional phase or preparation for adulthood then there is an inevitable tendency to view children and the manifestations of childhood as necessarily incomplete: literally immature. There is a hierarchy of significance and status that inevitably diminishes the outcomes and activities of children. The education system, in particular, places increasing importance on the education of young people as they get older – witness the relative funding of early years and post-compulsory education. The fact that this flies in the face of what we know of the importance of the cognitive development of very young children does nothing to change the way in which education policy prioritizes resources.

However, if Archard (2004) is correct and

> … in the modern view, childhood has its own characteristic needs and interests, and these have a value of their own. The modern conception of childhood can claim to be child-centred, to consider 'the child in the child' as Rousseau expressed it. (page 44)

then it becomes possible to argue for a model of childhood that recognizes and respects childhood as having value of itself. In particular, and crucially in the context of this book, it is important that we do not see children's spiritual and moral responses as partial, incomplete or naive versions of the proper (adult) version. The reality is, of course, that there is as much variation between adults as there is between adults and children. This is not to argue for a postmodern relativism in which everything has meaning, but rather to argue for recognition of the integrity and authenticity of any human being's response to the great questions. If a child's responses are personally meaningful and authentic (in other words, not just replicating adults' views in order to please them) then we can respect those responses as being valid. Of course, the scope, sophistication and motivation will change with age:

> Although some aspects of moral development, such as empathy for others, are present among pre-schoolers, at age five to six … the child is likely to adhere to moral rules in order to avoid punishment and simply conform to the superior power of adults. By the age of seven and eight, the child starts to make decisions based on self-interest, aware that each person has their own interests and that these will be different from his or her own. The major shift in this period, according to this model, is around age eight to nine, when there begins to be a clearer sense that making the 'right' decision and obeying moral laws is a matter of living up to what is expected of you by people important to you. There is the wish to be 'a good person' in one's own eyes and the eyes of others. (Schofield, 2006, cited on page 206 in Algate et al., 2006)

It does not seem unreasonable to argue that there are adults whose behaviour is determined by fear, power and the desire to please. Equally, many will recognize the totally negative experience described by McIntosh (2004):

> I grew up in a conservative and fundamentalist culture. In both primary and secondary school we had to learn whole chapters of the Bible by heart. As one of my friends from the village put it recently, 'Many of our teachers were halfway between the minister and the policeman.' Each morning, classes started with a mass recital of the question-and-answer doctrinal responses from the 1647 Westminster Shorter Catechism, the creed of Scots Presbyterianism. I still remember Question No. 1: 'What is the chief end of man?' The reply was: 'Man's chief end is to glorify God and enjoy Him forever.' And maybe I was daydreaming and missed it, but I can't remember anyone ever explaining to us infants what a 'chief end' actually was. (page 47)

What is clear is that from a very early age children have an inherent disposition to engage with fundamental questions about the purpose of living and the meaning of death. They are willing to engage with deep fears, recognize the 'monsters' in their lives and be capable of wonder, love and profound engagement with others. There are children who bear pain and face death with greater courage and dignity than adults; the spontaneous, open and trusting love of a child may be more authentic than the cynical, exploitative relationships of some adults.

> ... If we suppose that children live in conceptual worlds that are structurally different from ours, but that will naturally evolve into ours, how can we fail to be condescending toward children as moral agents?

> The condescension, though understandable, is unwarranted. One reason it is unwarranted is that ... later structures are not entirely unquestionable accomplishments, characteristically, they are problematic ...

Another reason such condescension is unwarranted is that children, in their simple directness, often bring us adults back to basics. Any developmental theory that rules out, on purely theoretical grounds, even the possibility that we adults may occasionally have something to learn, morally, from a child is, for that reason, defective, it is also morally offensive. (Matthews, 1994, pages 66–7)

In essence children's spiritual and moral development is self-legitimating – it does not have to be justified in terms of an apprenticeship for adult life nor seen as an incremental development in which the goal is effective adulthood. Legally, adulthood starts at 18 – morally and spiritually it can start before then or be delayed until long after. In fact, it might be possible that some of the spiritual experiences of childhood have greater integrity and authenticity than those of adults.

Hay (1998) describes research which asked adults to explore their childhood experiences of spirituality:

> ... People repeatedly spoke of them as having the greatest personal significance when they were contemplating their personal identity and the meaning of their lives. No doubt there had been a considerable development in the interpretation and perhaps embellishment of these experiences as the individual thought about them over the years ... vision of childhood could perhaps be locked out of awareness as we enter the secularized world of adult life. (pages 44–5)

It may be worth remembering that the presumed relative sophistication of adulthood may in fact be compromised by the need for conformity, to demonstrate autonomy and the need to be 'part of'. Sometimes the language and behaviour of childhood is more authentic and genuine than the posturing of adulthood.

On the day following a major security scare at British airports one of us was caught in the queue for security screening. While superficially polite and tolerant, there was a real sense of tension, anxiety and impatience – not helped by the fact that it was 5.30 a.m. A small child, perhaps three years old, tired and troubled, was adamantly refusing to pass through the detector. The parents' cajoling quickly turned to frustration; the child became increasingly distressed and obdurate; the queue became increasingly irritated; the security staff became more insistent – the child had to pass through on his own. Eventually, one of the security staff knelt down, opened her arms, smiled at the child and called him through – the child ran through and flung himself into her arms. Everybody in the queue smiled, laughed and said 'aaaah'. There was a palpable release of tension. It may well be that the child's reaction – fear followed by trust and acceptance – were more authentic than the behaviour of many of the adults present. Schooling can often infantilize, we need to be careful not to marginalize genuine responses to the world.

Happiness

If we consider all of the motivations potentially influencing human action and choice, the probability is that the one superordinate factor is happiness. We seek love, success, economic security and a whole range of other possible outcomes, to the extent that we perceive they will contribute to our happiness. Happiness is far more than the absence of grief and pain.

> Nor can there be any happiness without love. ... Hence love is transparent joy, its light, its known and acknowledged truth. This is ... the secret of wisdom and happiness: love exists only as joy and there is no joy other than love. (Comte-Sponville, 1996, page 253)

If parents are asked their hopes and aspirations for their children, and children are asked for their most fundamental ambitions, the chances are that happiness, directly or indirectly, will dominate the responses. The reason why we love and seek to be loved, why we are moral, why we strive for success and why we are spiritual beings is to secure happiness.

The founding fathers of the USA made 'life, liberty and the pursuit of happiness' the bedrock of their constitution. One of the dominant themes in ethics and political philosophy is the elusive concept of the 'greatest happiness of the greatest number'. In these contexts happiness is not just about the absence of pain; it is a highly positive state of deliberate and thoughtful engagement:

> Aristotle said that a life truly worth living is one that produces *eudaimonia*, the feeling of being 'watched over by a good angel' – an image he used figuratively, not in a literal religious sense. Most translations of this term render it in English as 'happiness', the contemporary meaning of which entirely subverts the strong, active connotation of *eudaimonia* as well-doing and well-being, as living flourishingly.
>
> To the best of *eudaimonic* people Aristotle gave the label *megalopsychos*, meaning 'great souled' … (Grayling, 2001, pages 72–3)

Martin (2005, pages 12–13) argues that it is possible to identify four elements of happiness:

- Pleasure – 'the presence of pleasant positive moods or emotions'.
- Absence of displeasure – 'the absence of unpleasant, negative moods or emotions'.
- Satisfaction – 'judging, on reflection, that you are satisfied with your life in general'.
- Virtue – 'for a life to be truly happy it must have some deeper purpose and meaning'.

If the negative definition is removed, happiness seems self-evident, but it is important to stress then there are three broad, positive components to living a happy life – it is one that has access to pleasure, provides satisfaction and is an expression of fundamental values being transferred into day-to-day experiences. Of course this definition is very broad and sweeping but does help to provide a generic context. In many ways it parallels the Every Child Matters agenda in English schools – a broad framework which creates a context for specific strategies. This topic will be returned to in the final section of this chapter but it is worth stressing at this stage that there can be no objectivity in this debate – happiness is a unique, subjective and highly personal phenomenon. That is why the development of spiritual and emotional literacy is so fundamental to learning, the possibility of happiness and the development of authentic people. An essential corollary of being happy is the ability to understand, communicate and so replicate that happiness.

Martin (2005, pages 48–71) goes on to elaborate the components of happiness; in other words, the means by which we might achieve fulfilment in our lives:

1. Connectedness: linked to other people through secure, loving and interdependent relationships.

2. Social and emotional competence: social skills and emotional literacy to manage self and relationships with others.

3. Freedom from excessive anxiety: the absence of tension and stress.

4. Communication skills: the ability to exchange ideas, information and emotions in a meaningful way.

5. Engagement in meaningful activity: active engagement in active purposeful and rewarding activity.

6. A sense of control: a sense of being able to take decisions and exercise choices in one's life.

7. A sense of purpose and meaning: the existence of long-term goals that are challenging, significant and motivating.

8. Resilience: the ability to 'bounce-back', overcome difficulties and maintain a positive outlook.

9. Self-esteem: having a positive sense of one's value as a person – liking yourself.

10. Optimum: a sense of well-being and a generally positive disposition.

11. Outward focus: being extrovert rather than introvert, concerned with the world rather than morbid self-absorption.

12. Present and future mindedness: the disposition to focus on and enjoy the present rather than dwell on the past and avoiding an artificial belief in a better future.

13. Humour: laughter and fun are good for us.

14. Playfulness: play through interaction and engagement, for example games and sport.

15. Wisdom: a personal understanding of the world and the ability to learn from experience.

16. Freedom from excessive materialism: the recognition that financial wealth and possessions do little to create sustainable happiness.

17. Experiencing flow: activities which lead to absolute engagement, absorption and focus.

This is an intimidating list and it would be blatant nonsense to use it as an inventory for managing a life or to try to prioritize it and create a 'curriculum for happiness'. At the same time, this list does provide a set of criteria which can inform the debate about the components of an effective and fulfilling life – not least for children and young people.

Three common factors seem to unite Martin's challenging criteria: the centrality of relationships and engagement with others; a clear sense of purpose; and direction and a positive disposition. What links these three is that they are matters of personal perception and derived from a sense of self:

> In fact happiness depends on your inner life as much as on your outer circumstances. Through education and practice, it is possible to improve your inner life – to accept yourself better and to feel more for others. In most of us there is a deep positive force, which can be liberated if we can overcome our negative thoughts. To develop this inner strength of character should be a major goal of education. (Layard, 2005, page 230)

The development of an 'inner life' is fundamentally concerned with spiritual and moral development. At its most basic, human happiness is rooted in the development of the existential self and this is a product of a coherent, integrated and systematic approach to educating children in the broadest sense:

> … it is possible to envision an education that places understanding centrally in the curriculum. Once this decisive step has been taken, it becomes possible – despite many obstacles – to move in the direction of greater understanding. One must activate two powerful allies: the disciplines of knowledge that have developed painstakingly over the centuries, and the habits in which students work regularly and determinedly to master knowledge and skills and to activate them in the service of understanding. The distinguished British educator Paul Hirst once argued that disciplines do not train the mind; rather, they let us see what it is to have a mind. And that is certainly a goal worth aiming for and, perhaps, even an end to which one might meaningfully devote one's life. (Gardner, 2006a, page 158)

If we are to educate for understanding, it would seem that we need a model of education which starts with the child (rather than the curriculum, school or teacher) and has at its core an overarching focus on happiness, and recognizes that happiness is significantly determined by spiritual and moral development.

Education

In the most negative sense, hospitals bureaucratize health in the same way that schools bureaucratize education and learning. Of course there are very good reasons for this – largely economic and organizational but also concerned with issues of equity and access. However, we have become so habituated into thinking that hospitals are about health that we forget that they are largely places of the last resort – when all else has failed. It would be a very different world if as much energy, resource, professionalism and skill was invested in the prevention of illness rather than its cure.

Schooling has become so reified that we often forget that it is one element in education, and that personal success (however defined) is the product of many complex interacting variables. It is possible to identify three factors that are the most influential in determining a young person's life chances through their impact on the broad range of educational outcomes:

- Social factors: poverty, social class, community and family life.
- Personal factors: aptitude, ability, engagement, motivation.
- School factors: effective learning and teaching, a culture of achievement.

There will be significant variation in the relative importance of these variables; personal success will be the result of a complex interaction between them. What is clear is that the social and personal factors will always be more significant than the school factors. A child living in economic security, in an effective family, within a positive community, will always be relatively advantaged compared to the child living in the negative corollary of these factors. The success of a school will always be the product of positive social and personal factors; the failure of a school will likewise be the result, to a very significant degree, of those factors.

It is therefore important to recognize the limits of schooling and to stress the importance of understanding the broader implications of educating, especially in the context of spiritual and moral development. The essential components of schooling and educating are shown in the Figure 2.1.

Schooling	Educating
Linear	Adaptive
Fragmented	Holistic
Curriculum content	Learning for understanding
Information transmission	Knowledge creation
Quantifiable outcomes	Qualitative outcomes
Structures	Relationships

Figure 1.1 Schooling and educating (adapted from West-Burnham et al., 2007, page 41)

It is possible to find rich educational experiences in schools – the figure creates an artificial polarity, the reality is never so extreme – it is better to see the relationship as a continuum.

What is clear is that many schools, for largely externally generated reasons, for example accountability, feel it necessary to focus on the outcomes of schooling: the delivery of the curriculum in order to maximize quantifiable outcomes. If spiritual and moral development is to be more than the delivery of information about the world's religions and the specification of rules about behaviour, then it has to engage with educational practices. The importance of this is recognized by the National Curriculum.

> During key stage 2 pupils learn about themselves as growing and changing individuals with their own experiences and ideas, and as members of their communities. They become more mature, independent and self-confident. They learn about the wider world and the interdependence of communities within it. They develop their sense of social justice and moral responsibility and begin to understand that their own choices and behaviour can affect local, national or global issues and political and social institutions. They learn how to take part more fully in school and community activities. As they begin to develop into young adults, they face the changes of puberty and transfer to secondary school with support and encouragement from their school. They learn how to make more confident and informed choices about their own health and environment; to take more responsibility, individually and as a group, for their own learning; and to resist bullying. (QCA, 1999)

The importance of holistic approaches to personal growth and development is also reflected in the outcomes of Every Child Matters (ECM). What is so important about ECM is that it represents the first integrated and systematic approach, in England, to the *education* of the whole child. The five outcomes of ECM can be seen as an explicit articulation of a child's entitlement to a range of social and educational outcomes. The five elements of ECM are:

- be healthy
- stay safe
- enjoy and achieve
- make a positive contribution
- achieve economic well-being.

They can only be achieved if there is a broad-based recognition of the contribution of spiritual and moral development. The implementation of ECM has tended to focus, quite properly, on a range of strategies that increase engagement with families and communities and extending the range of services that schools provide: yet even the most superficial reading of ECM points to the need for the policies and strategies to be underpinned by explicit cross-referencing to spiritual and moral development.

Although there is, quite understandably but sadly, no reference to happiness in the ECM strategies, it can be argued that a child who achieves all the outcomes will, in essence, be a happy person. It is perhaps a lost opportunity not to have human happiness as the overarching rationale for ECM, although it does raise the daunting prospect of human happiness being reduced to minimalist, reductionist and quantifiable performance indicators.

In many ways the education system of England is going through a transitional phase – moving from the narrow focus on outcomes of schooling that dominated the 1990s to a broader view of what comprises effective education. Some of these are derived from policy; some grow out of the professionalism and creativity of teachers and school leaders. Taylor and Pite (2006) capture the potential impact of these changes:

> The *Common Core of Skills and Knowledge for the Children's Workforce (2005)* addresses the broad issues of joined-up working and the importance of professionals from different backgrounds developing and sharing common practitioner values. In this article we would like to suggest that two other elements will be central to our route map. These are:
>
> • a focus on effective learning – this is at the heart of improving life chances and central to the purpose of the children's workforce
>
> • building capacity to sustain improvement in schools must be seen in the light of much larger understandings about the nature of sustainability – not only in the context of the five outcomes but also in the context of our moral purpose and responsibility for our own survival. (pages 13–14)

In their subsequent discussion of the centrality of effective learning they demonstrate that:

> Current expectations of learners can be found in Ofsted's *Handbook for Inspecting Secondary Schools* (2003). Two questions are asked: 'are pupils enterprising and willing to take responsibility?' and 'do pupils develop the capacity to work independently and collaboratively?'
>
> Digging deeper we find behavioural indicators designed to help such judgements:
>
> • pupils are able to handle uncertainty and respond positively to change
>
> • pupils think and act creatively, use critical thinking, suggest ways forward and solve problems for themselves
>
> • pupils are able to tackle new tasks willingly and are confident in finding their own solutions to problems
>
> • pupils are curious and want to learn
>
> • pupils make reasonable assessments of risks when trying new things
>
> • pupils are committed to improvement and making a difference
>
> • pupils take responsibility for their work and do their best
>
> • pupils work fruitfully in collaboration with others.
>
> The school is also expected to enable a pupil to develop self-awareness. (ibid., page 15)

This topic is dealt with in much more detail in Chapter 4, but it is important to stress at this stage that the nurturing and support of spiritual and moral development can only really happen in the context of a broad-based view of education, one that:

> ... helps children to become happy, healthy and successful people, both in childhood and throughout their lives. But it must be the right sort of education – one that develops children's social skills, resilience and wisdom. The right sort of education should also leave children with a lifelong love of learning. Academic skills can be acquired surprisingly quickly if the teaching is good and the child is ready and motivated to learn. Meanwhile, leave them some time and space to play. (Martin, 2005, page 229)

In summary, it would seem that an approach to education which (a) respects the integrity of childhood, (b) seeks to enhance the possibility of happiness and (c) aspires to educate the person rather than school the pupil has the following characteristics:

- A focus on the development of the person and respect for individual differences.
- A curriculum that recognizes the full range of human experience and potential.
- The development of a range of cognitive, social and emotional skills, strategies and behaviours.
- The creation of opportunities to explore the full dimensions of what it means to be human.
- Communities, families and schools that model the desired qualities.

2 Education and spirituality

In this book we understand spirituality as a fundamental component of what it means to be fully human. Spirituality is a basic disposition which characterizes us as sentient beings. We recognize, and respect, that spirituality is often associated with religious practice and is an essential expression of all the great faiths, but we would argue that the manifestations of spirituality are not unique to these faiths. They have numerous manifestations in human relationships, the arts and the many expressions of human identity. It is not our intention to provide a manual in how to be a better member of a particular faith, but rather to explore the most elemental human instinct to engage with that which is non-material, timeless and transcends the everyday boundaries of human experience and existence. This is a fundamental imperative found in every faith, culture and era, and is expressed in music, poetry, the arts and literature, and given expression in wonderfully diverse ways. It is an experience available to all, even rats and moles:

> 'It's gone!' sighed the Rat, sinking back in his seat again. 'So beautiful and strange and new! Since it was to end so soon, I almost wish I had never heard it. For it has roused a longing in me that is pain, and nothing seems worth while but just to hear that sound once more and go on listening to it for ever. No! There it is again!' he cried, alert once more. Entranced, he was silent for a long space, spellbound. 'Now it passes on and I begin to lose it,' he said presently. 'O, Mole! the beauty of it! . . .' (Grahame, 1994, page 143)

Grahame's description of Ratty and Mole's meeting with the Piper at the Gates of Dawn captures the sense of transcendence that is often associated with spiritual experiences. However, this is only one dimension of what it means to be a spiritual being. There are many examples of human activity that can be regarded as spiritual which are not limited to the transcendent but rather enable transcendence.

Engaging with the spiritual is the process of coming to terms with a number of questions and, if not actually answering them, learning how to come to terms with the challenges they offer. Such questions might include:

- Who am I?
- Who might I become?
- What do I believe?

These are the most fundamental questions that we can ask; the very act of acknowledging them opens the doors of spiritual development and growth. While they may carry connotations of existentialist angst, they are in fact elemental to any notion of emerging as an autonomous, authentic person. Although the form of the questions might change, as might the answers, they are as relevant to the five-year-old as to the 50-year-old. At all stages of development, spiritual growth is complex, delicate and fragile. Becoming a confident spiritual being is a multifaceted and deeply personal adventure. We see spirituality as a process: a journey in response to these questions and the ability to engage with them as a key outcome of effective education and learning.

For many, this spiritual journey is movement towards union with God. However, for many others it is the journey itself that is significant. What both share is the development of self: a growth in confidence and clarity about 'what it means to be me'.

Therefore, as a starting point, we offer a definition of spirituality which informs the rest of our discussion.

> **Spirituality is the journey to find an authentic, unified and profound understanding of the existential self which informs action, sustains hope and enables personal transformation.**

The components of this definition will be discussed throughout this chapter but at this stage it is perhaps worth highlighting the key ones:

- *Spirituality is the journey* – spirituality is a process rather than a destination; it is emergent and linked directly to learning. It is not related to age, status or ability.
- *An authentic, unified and profound understanding* – a holistic sense of what it means to be a person who has all the elements integrated, balanced and mutually reinforcing.
- *The existential self* – the most profound sense of who I am.
- *Informs action* – guides me as a social being.
- *Sustains hope* – enables me to continue the journey.
- *Enables personal transformation* – so that I have the potential to become who I might be.

Spirituality is thus the means by which, in many wonderfully varied ways, humanity seeks to respond to the great existential questions regarding purpose, life and death, beauty and creativity. Answers can be found in religion, science, the arts, relationships and community. What is needed is the capacity and resilience to engage with the questions. Wangari Maathai, the Nobel Peace Prize winning campaigner for environmental reform, uses trees as a metaphor for the fundamental elements in life:

> Trees have been an essential part of my life and have provided me with many lessons. Trees are living symbols of peace and hope. A tree has roots in the soil yet reaches to the sky. It tells us that in order to aspire we need to be grounded, and that no matter how high we go it is from our roots that we draw sustenance. It is a reminder to all of us who have had success that we cannot forget where we came from. It signifies that no matter how powerful we become in government or how many awards we receive, our power and strength and our ability to reach our goals depend on the people, those whose work remains unseen, who are the soil out of which we grow, the shoulders on which we stand. (2007, page 293)

Modes of spirituality

Spirituality is multifaceted, yet it is often seen only in terms of prayer and mysticism. Equally, spirituality is not about the liturgy of the churches even though prayer and the liturgy are powerful routes into spirituality for some. We want to argue that spirituality is best seen as a component of the full range of human experiences. Spirituality grows out of our lives and, at the same time, extends them and creates new possibilities for growth as a person.

The following typology is derived from Kessler (2000) and Richardson (1996). This typology stresses the multiple routes into spirituality: each is valid, each significant – their status being determined by the extent to which they are meaningful to the individual. Spirituality may be found in the search for *self, truth, social justice, community, beauty* and *love.*

Spirituality as the search for self:

- the journey to personal understanding and acceptance
- the quest for selfhood, becoming authentic
- profound learning, becoming wise
- aspiration, growth and hope.

The search for self is one of the most abiding themes of spirituality. It is a universal concern found in every faith and philosophy across the ages and in every culture. It is a dominant theme in art, literature and poetry; it is found in the lyrics of the most banal pop song and in the greatest masterpieces of the Renaissance. At its most elemental, this is a search for identity and purpose, a sense of engagement and the basis for all other interactions.

The spiritual journey in search of self is the attempt to understand one's value and significance as an autonomous and authentic human being, as a child of God, a social entity or an astonishing product of the evolutionary process.

What seems fundamental to this journey is the discovery and development of the worth and dignity of the person in their own right, and the assiduous cultivation of that person over time. Crucially enabling the child to be comfortable and confident in who they are, valued for who they are and seeing their potential for growth.

This dimension of spirituality leads us to seeking answers to the following questions:

- What is it that makes 'me' me?
- What is left, if I am not described as 'child of …' or 'friend of …'?
- How do I know who I am?
- How do my parents, siblings and friends describe me?
- Who do I want to be in five years, ten years?
- How would I describe myself?
- What has made me who I am?
- Do I like myself?
- When do I feel most comfortable being me?
- What do I need from others?
- What happens to *me* when *I* die?
- What gives me hope?

Spirituality as the search for truth involves:

- holistic understanding
- mystical union
- transcendence
- the search for wisdom.

The journey towards truth is fraught with problems and possibilities – not least because there are so many alternative versions available. Such a journey might follow the path of the Buddha or that of the theoretical physicist. The very possibility of truth might be questioned by the postmodernist. The Christian theologian and the humanist philosopher might disagree about the nature of the journey but will use remarkably similar intellectual strategies. There is a profound human predisposition to seek certainty – the idea that there is an objective truth is deeply reassuring. The possibility that there might not be truth can be disturbing and distressing.

The great mystics in all religions found truth in a complete union with God. For the scientist it is the need to find scientifically valid explanations for 'life, the universe and everything'. Philosophers and lawgivers have sought to create universally applicable systems.

Fundamental to all of these approaches is a deep sense of the possibility of solving problems, finding answers and improving. There is a basic human need to believe in the possibility of transformation and even transcendence – moving into higher levels of engagement and understanding. Central to the search for truth is the possibility of holistic understanding, unity, oneness – the possibility of coherence and completeness.

The search for truth, or the Truth, might involve the following questions:

- Why am I here?
- Is there a unifying purpose to our lives?
- Are there answers or only better questions?
- Is it possible to find completeness and unity in this life?
- How do I make sense of what is happening to me?
- Who can help me on this journey? How do I know I can trust them?
- Does accepting somebody else's solution mean I stop asking questions?
- Do I accept who I am or search for a better me?

Spirituality as the search for social justice involves:

- social idealism
- living an ethical life
- sacrifice and duty
- anger at injustice.

Spirituality as the search for social justice is about the imperative to turn principle into practice. It has its roots in social idealism, the belief that social life can be transformed through social actions. It is often expressed through anger resulting from seeing the reasons of poverty, injustice, prejudice, intolerance – anything that challenges our deeply held beliefs about what it means to be human. This is very much about spirituality – as action translating beliefs into social engagement which often involves personal sacrifice, danger and discomfort.

In this context the spiritual can blend into the political – at its simplest it is giving to the poor and demonstrating against poverty. But it can also involve living and working with the poor, creating work for the poor and abandoning a comfortable life for one of discomfort. As Aung San Suu Kyi, the leader of the democracy movement in Burma, expresses it:

The 'power of the powerless' as Václav Havel said. I think power comes from within. If you have confidence in what you are doing and you are shored up by the belief that what you are doing is right, that in itself constitutes power, and this power is very important when you are trying to achieve something. If you don't believe in what you are doing your actions will lack credibility. However hard you try, inconsistencies will appear. (cited in Clements and Aung, 1997, page 119)

Spirituality is essential to the search for social justice in that it is the source of compassion and anger, it provides courage and consistency, and it ensures sustainability. Those who commit themselves to social action often do so on the basis of anger at injustice, a belief in human dignity and other moral imperatives – it is the depth of spiritual engagement that moves a person from armchair indignation to direct action, from sending an online donation to personal engagement.

The search for social justice can raise a range of question and issues:

- Have I come to help or be part of the struggle?
- What does it mean to be truly human?
- How do I demonstrate my commitment to social justice and equity in my daily life?
- Am I genuinely inclusive?
- What are the boundaries to my commitment?
- Is my anger and indignation creative and positive?
- How authentic is my commitment?

Spirituality as the search for community involves:

- service to others
- building trust
- living in community
- connections, networks, engagement
- growth through work
- joy, happiness and celebration.

Spirituality as the search for community is one of the most basic expressions of our higher selves. As the Dalai Lama expresses it:

Simply make clear the essential human values: a warm heart, a sense of caring for one another. Make these things clear. These values can be taught without referring to a religious point of view. They can be taught using secular arguments. For example, basic to human nature is that we are social animals. We can't survive as single persons, without the company of others. (1999, page 88)

An almost identical message comes from a totally different cultural and religious tradition: from Archbishop Desmond Tutu:

> We say a person is a person through other persons. We don't come fully formed into the world. We learn how to think, how to walk, how to speak, how to behave, indeed how to be human from other human beings. We need other human beings in order to be human. We are made for togetherness, we are made for family for fellowship, to exist in a tender network of interdependence … This is how you have *ubuntu* – you care, you are hospitable, you're gentle, you're compassionate and concerned. (cited in Battle, 1997, page 65)

The Southern African concept of *ubuntu* captures the essence of spirituality as the search for community, seeking to transcend the pettiness and potential negativity of human relationships to achieve authentic sharing of our lives to maximize our potential.

Religious grouping does seem to have an advantage in creating community. In its most extreme form, the monastery or the church congregation or the informal networks, or religious groups seem better at creating a sense of unity, common purpose and social interdependence. (Although, it has been said, monasteries can be highly political places and the Christian churches have a history of schism.)

However, what makes the religious community work is available to other social groupings – supporters of a football team, a military unit, a project team in a business, an orchestra et cetera, et cetera. Paradoxically we are more likely to maximize our potential as a person in a community than in isolation. We are products of our evolutionary history – there is a biological imperative and moral dimension that determines how we are together.

The strength, cohesion and resilience of a community are directly related to the extent to which it has social capital – the 'superglue' that holds a community together.

> Churches provide an important incubator for civic skills, civic norms, community interests, and civic recruitment. Religiously active men and women learn to give speeches, run meetings, manage disagreements, and bear administrative responsibility. They also befriend others who are in turn likely to recruit them into other forms of community activity. In part for these reasons, churchgoers are substantially more likely to be involved in secular organizations, to vote and participate politically in other ways, and to have deeper informal social connections.
>
> Regular worshipers and people who say that religion is very important to them are much more likely than other people to visit friends, to entertain at home, to attend club meetings, and to belong to sports groups; professional and academic societies; school service groups; youth groups; service clubs; hobby or garden clubs; literary, art, discussion and study groups; school fraternities and sororities; farm organizations; political clubs; nationality groups; and other miscellaneous groups. (Putnam, 2000, pages 66–7)

It may be that other groups in society can learn from religious groups – shared spirituality makes for healthy communities.

The following questions may help an exploration of the relationship between spirituality and community:

- To what extent are my values aligned with those of the various communities I belong to?
- How much time do we spend as a community exploring, articulating and consolidating our shared beliefs?
- What images, symbols and rituals help us to understand our shared identity?
- How rich are our networks, dialogue and communication?
- How much trust is there in our community? How is it manifested?
- To what extent do people share, cooperate and collaborate?
- How much voluntary activity is there?
- What is done to ensure the long-term viability of the community?
- How do we celebrate being a community?

Spirituality as beauty includes:

- creativity in the arts
- engagement with the natural world
- performance.

For many, one of the most powerful ways into spirituality is through the creation and contemplation of beauty expressed through the visual arts, music, poetry and the natural world. The possibilities offered by music seem boundless and the emotional and spiritual response to music enables people to 'fall into themselves unknowingly'. This can be found in the football crowd singing 'You'll Never Walk Alone' and 800 singers learning, rehearsing and performing Tallis' 'Spem in Alium' in a day. Performing and listening to music are both powerful entry points and it would be arrogant in the extreme to argue that the music of Monteverdi is more spiritually significant that the music of Cole Porter, John Coltrane or the Beatles. There are many pathways to spiritual engagement.

In the same way, the visual arts offer profound possibilities for spirituality both through the creative act and reflecting on that act. In his discussion of the painter Kandinsky, Spivey (2005) highlights the possibilities and problems of approaching the spiritual through music and art:

> Musicians are to be envied. They have at their disposal a means of expressing spiritual states; a means of expression that is independent of nature, that is its own construct. Some

musicians may take inspiration from a song thrush piping in the woods, or a drumming of thunder. But music does not *need* those models. Its sounds can have a life all their own. Art, by contrast – well, art seems to be reliant upon not only nature, but a whole universe of objects … Could art never, then, operate like music: take the human soul soaring into the bliss of transcendence, above and away from the things of the world? (page 251)

In fact, of course, what the visual arts can do is inspire, challenge and, crucially, stimulate reflection on the physical world. In the same way that a landscape photographer can capture a vista in a way that creates new meaning, significance and insight.

The act of creating a photograph is, potentially, as spiritual a process as the reflection on that photograph. So, with music, dance and theatre, creating, performing and observing all offer opportunities to explore and create meaning, develop understanding and inform action. Much the same is true of engagement with the natural world.

Looking through a microscope and a telescope both offer opportunities for discovery, wonder and challenge. Landscape has enormously evocative powers, being by the sea, in a favourite wood or seeing animals in the wild can all provoke profound emotional and spiritual responses. The nursery school that ensures that every child has the opportunity to hold a newborn lamb is creating possibilities for a wide range of spiritual insights:

Our relation to the universe community involves us in the broadest context that the human spirit can understand. … We are members of the universe community that makes of us the stuff of stars. The universe is the primary sacred reality. … All peoples, from time immemorial, have taken a vital interest in their relationship to the universe. The most wonderful myths have been spun by diverse peoples all over the earth celebrating our origin story within their understanding. The sense of the expansiveness of the universe is food for the soul. The awesome grandeur of it all leaves us both breathless and energized.

… Our souls are nourished within the earth's matrix. It is a matrix that exhibits incredible variety and enormous grandeur. The earth's landscape is rich nourishment for the human spirit. (O'Sullivan, 1999, pages 261–2)

To see a group of children from an impoverished urban environment exploring a wood for the first time is to understand the potential of context as a vehicle for personal understanding. In a very real sense, engagement with the natural world is the human issue – our ability to destroy our planet might be seen as the result of a lack of connectedness:

These, then, are some of the basic principles of ecology – interdependence, recycling, partnership, flexibility, diversity, and, as a consequence of all those sustainability. … the survival of humanity will depend on our ecological literacy, on our ability to understand these principles of ecology and live accordingly. (Capra, 1996, page 295)

For Capra the implications of this position are clear:

- Spiritual experience is an experience of aliveness of mind and body as a unity. Moreover, this experience of unity transcends not only the separation of mind and body, but also the separation of self and world. The central awareness in these spiritual moments is a profound sense of oneness with all, a sense of belonging to the universe as a whole.
- This sense of oneness with the natural world is fully borne out by the new scientific conception of life.
- We belong to the universe, we are at home in it, and this experience of belonging can make our lives profoundly meaningful. (Capra, 2002, pages 59–60)

This leads us to consider:

- What opportunities do you create for yourself and others to be creative?
- What music moves you? How do you use this music to explore your personal understanding?
- What works of art are significant in your life? What do they tell you about your spiritual growth?
- When and where was the last time you were overwhelmed by a manifestation of the natural world? Why did it overwhelm you?
- Is there a special place that is highly resonant and significant in your life? When was the last time you went there?
- How open are you to new possibilities of engaging with beauty?

Spirituality as love involves:

- the unconditional love of another
- the acceptance of love
- love through significant relationships.

For many children the experience of loving and being loved is their first real experience of a higher-order transcendent relationship. It is the first engagement with what, for many, is one of the pivotal, defining characteristics of what makes us human. Love defines lives, changes lives and provides reasons for living and dying. Love in our lives can range from the mysteries of the love of God to the self-denying love of friendship. From the safety and solidity of long-term married love to the brief passion. In every case, love defines both those who love and are loved.

Few of us have experienced unconditional love. Within the human context, there is always some kind of price to pay. Rightly or wrongly we feel we must earn or merit the love of others. It is no easy art, to do the loving thing. The profound poet Rainer Maria Rilke was well aware of this truth.

For one human being to love another human being:
That is perhaps
The most difficult task that has been entrusted to us,
The ultimate task, the final test and proof,
The work for which all work is merely preparation.

(O'Leary, 2001, pages 84–5)

Love is the universal experience and figures in every faith and philosophy – a child's first abstract articulation will often be about love. It is the area that we are simultaneously most and least articulate throughout our lives. A pivotal manifestation of love as spirituality is in the universal phenomenon of friendship. Friendship, in its many forms, may well be one of the most powerful expressions of spirituality and, simultaneously, a crucial vehicle to develop spiritual understanding.

… soul friends' qualified need of each other, in the sense of respecting each others' individuality, means that they do not mind being physically apart for periods of time. … Alternatively, soul friends understand one another to the extent that they trust one another implicitly: when they befriend others, if to a lesser degree, the seeds of jealously are not sown between them.

Deep respect. Implicit trust. No distorting neediness. Even a first look at soul friendship shows that it is nothing if not an exceptional state. (Vernon, 2005, pages 146–7)

In his exploration of Celtic spirituality, O'Donohue (1997) focuses on the *anam cara*, the 'soul friend' experience which:

… opens a friendship that is not wounded or limited by separation or distance. Such friendship can remain alive even when the friends live far way from each other. Because they have broken through the barriers of personal egoism to the soul level, the unity of their souls is not easily severed. (page 31)

It is difficult to conceive of spiritual growth that is not rooted in friendship and significant relationships which reflect the many manifestations of love. The most effective learning relationships will be based in a mutual regard and respect that is a shallow manifestation of love. It is a sad reflection of our times that it is difficult to envisage a school articulating love as its core purpose – yet love will be the defining experience of everyone involved in the work of the school.

It seems inappropriate to ask a multitude of questions about love, analysis might destroy its essential qualities of mystery and wonder – perhaps it is best to simply ask:

• Do you know in how many ways you are loved?

It would be wrong to see these six components of spirituality as alternative pathways – see them rather as a complex network of paths – some broad and well trodden, others neglected and overgrown. All are available; culture, context and personal disposition will guide us to which pathways are best for us. Sometimes, if we are lucky, several pathways will merge into a clear and easy road to follow. Sometimes we can spend a lifetime trying to find a path that allows us to travel forwards.

A key function of the teacher, the guide, the mentor is to help us understand what paths might be available and how we might start the journey. Our ability to engage in any kind of spiritual journey or development will be significantly determined by what Zohar and Marshall (2000) describe as spiritual intelligence (SQ):

> Neither IQ [intelligence quota] nor EQ [emotional intelligence quota], separately or in combination, is enough to explain the full complexity of human intelligence nor the vast richness of the human soul and imagination … SQ [spiritual quota] allows human beings to be creative, to change the rules and to alter situations. It allows us to play with the boundaries, to play an 'infinite game'. SQ gives us our ability to discriminate. It gives us our moral sense, and ability to temper rigid rules with understanding and compassion and an equal ability to see when compassion and understanding have their limits. We use SQ to wrestle with questions of good and evil and to envision unrealized possibilities – to dream, to aspire, to raise ourselves out of the mud. (page 5)

Zohar and Marshall identify the indicators of spiritual intelligence as follows:

• The capacity to be flexible.
• A high degree of self-awareness.
• A capacity to face and use suffering.
• A capacity to face and transcend pain.
• The quality of being inspired by vision and values.
• A reluctance to cause unnecessary harm.
• A tendency to see connections.
• A marked tendency to ask 'why?' or 'what if?' questions.
• The facility to work against convention. (ibid., page 15)

To this list we would add the following:

- A capacity for unconditional love.
- The ability to see beyond the here and now.
- A passion to create and share meaning.
- A capacity for wonder.

This list is profoundly challenging because it moves us out of the areas of human activity that we know and are potentially comfortable with – the cognitive and the emotional. Spiritual growth and development can never be a purely intellectual process nor is it understood through emotional or interpersonal intelligence. Both are necessary components of spiritual growth, but there is an additional dimension which is described in the list above.

Consider the following cases:

- The 18-month-old baby who spontaneously starts to feed her twin sister who has lost both hands as the result of a viral infection.
- The ten-year-old boy, who nurses his terminally ill mother, runs the household, cares for younger siblings and maintains attendance and progress at school.
- The orphaned refugee who maintains her dignity and hope, and continues to study so as to return to her native country 'and be of service'.
- The terminally ill child who remains buoyant and optimistic, radiating happiness to those around her.

In each case there is a set of qualities, a deep humanity which cannot be explained by intelligence or social skills – in a generic sense this is what we mean by spirituality. These are the qualities that transcend the normal patterns of behaviour and social expectations. The language that we use to describe such qualities will include words such as:

altruism

empathy

courage

dignity

sensitivity

caring

compassion

hope

joy

service.

Spirituality and authenticity

Everything that has been written so far in this chapter points to spirituality as the expression of the self. However, there is, as always, the possibility that individuals might use the language and/or behaviours of spirituality in a superficial or gratuitous way, in other words their spirituality is superficial or formulaic. Obvious examples are those who attend a church service but see no relationship to their daily lives, or those who happily donate to charity but fail to address the needs of family or neighbours.

The issue is the extent that a person's spiritual journey is authentic. This is the difference between 'do as I say' and 'do as I do'. Authenticity is about consistency and trust; it is about the movement from superficial observance, ritualized performance and spirituality by association to internalization and personal change through learning.

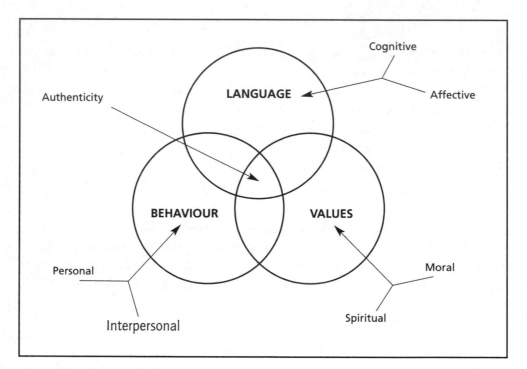

Figure 2.1 Developing authenticity

Figure 2.1 shows the relationship between personal values, language and behaviour. The more these elements are integrated – the more the circles overlap – the greater is the level of personal authenticity. The higher the level of synchronicity between what a person believes, how that belief informs their language and the extent to which his or her behaviour is consistent with that language the higher the level of authenticity. The chances are that the people we most respect, admire and are willing to listen to and follow are those with the greatest authenticity.

> Being authentic is knowing ourselves and being ourselves as we engage with others … no playing roles, no acting, no fulfilling the expectations of others. We are actually and exactly who we are. Nothing false, noting imitative, nothing imaginary. Being authentic means not hiding behind a mask, not faking what we think or feel, not using spin to promote a sanitized version of the truth. Being authentic is living with honesty and integrity. It is being transparent and congruent, matching inner reality with its outward experience. (Moxley, 2000, page 126)

Taylor (1991) places authenticity at the heart of personal growth and development:

> There is a certain way of being human that is *my* way. I am called upon to live my life in this way, and not in imitation of anyone else's. But this gives a new importance to being true to myself. If I am not, I miss the point of my life. I miss what being human is for *me*.

> Being true to myself means being true to my own originality, and that is something only I can articulate and discover. In articulating it, I am also defining myself. I am realizing a potentiality that is properly my own. This is the background of understanding to the modern ideal of authenticity, and to the goals of self-fulfilment or self-realization in which it is usually couched. This is the background that gives moral force to the culture of authenticity, including its most degraded, absurd, or trivialized forms. It is what gives sense to the idea of 'doing your own thing' or 'finding your own fulfilment.' (pages 28–9)

Being authentic is resisting the pressure to conform, rejecting the glib certainties, and having the courage to reject and refuse that which is unworthy or denigrates the person. Morality tells us what is right or wrong, good or bad. Spirituality gives us the reserves and resources to make and live with our choices.

Authenticity implies depth, resilience and sustainability. The development of the spiritual might be seen as creating 'reservoirs of hope'. Think of a dam across a deep and wide valley. Behind the dam is a reservoir. When necessary, the gates of the dam are opened and the power of the water is used to generate electricity; when the demand falls, the gates are closed and the reservoir is able to refill itself from the streams and rivers that feed into it. High demand will cause the levels of the reservoir to fall to critical levels.

Think now of a personal reservoir of hope and how, on some days, demand is high. We would argue that it is the spiritual life that refills the personal reservoir. All of the different elements of spirituality described in this chapter have the potential to refill personal reservoirs. Spiritual development is about ensuring that the streams and rivers are available to replenish and renew the reservoir. An empty reservoir means a life without hope and this limits our potential to be fully human, for Rabbi Jonathan Sacks:

Hope ... is what empowers us to take risks, to offer commitment, to give love, to bring new life into the world, to comfort the afflicted, to lift the fallen, to begin great undertakings, to live by our ideals. It is to be found in families and communities, in the great religious traditions and certainties of their humanist counterparts. It is sustained by them, as they are sustained by it. As so much in our world, privately, nationally and globally, becomes uncertain, it is the best way, perhaps the only way, of retaining our sense of the underlying goodness of the world and the miraculous gift of life itself. (2000, page 267)

3 Morality and education

There seems to be an overwhelming consensus that one of the most basic functions of any education system is to transmit, imbue and engage children with the prevailing morality of the society in which they live. There is less agreement on what that morality should be and how it might best be transmitted. Plato, in *The Republic*, was quite unequivocal about both what should be taught and how it should be taught. Such was the importance of moral education for Plato that he believed that censorship was justifiable. Lickona, in discussing the case for values education, comments that:

> Realising that smart and good are not the same, wise societies since the time of Plato have made moral education a deliberate aim of schooling. They have educated for character as well as intellect, decency as well as literacy, virtue as well as knowledge. They have tried to form citizens who will use their intelligence to benefit others as well as themselves, who will try to build a better world. (1992, page 6)

By this account moral education is essentially aspirational activity – seeking to create 'a better world' but at the same time it has to be pragmatic. Barber (1997) states that:

> The only moral communities to which all young people are entitled – indeed compelled – to belong is to the school. ... If we want young people to learn the rules of living and working in communities – how to solve differences of opinion, how to respect a variety of beliefs, how to make collective decisions in a democratic society, and so on – then these must feature in the curriculum of schools. (pages 187–8)

Moral education is important because it is a pivotal activity in creating the optimum society. However, even in ancient Athens, what that society might look like was contentious – witness the execution of Plato's teacher, Socrates, for subverting the young. One of the consequences of open and democratic societies is that people have options: are able to choose how they live. As societies become more complex and sophisticated so it becomes increasingly difficult to be confident about what model of morality should be taught. One of the challenges facing school leaders and teachers in this context is coming to terms with an ethically pluralist society, where there is no dominant, authoritative view, and where choices are perceived as contingent and relative.

A central precept of this book is that exercising moral choice, understanding and living with the consequences of that choice and behaving in a consistent way is challenging for any human being. Therefore, morality has to be underpinned by spirituality, as described in Chapter 2. These two elements might be seen as being in a symbiotic relationship: mutually reinforcing and sustaining each other. In one sense, spirituality can be seen as the source of morality, in another case it can be seen as the conscience – the benchmark for the choices that we all make on a daily basis. Spirituality helps to move moral behaviour from pragmatic and instrumental actions to deeply embedded beliefs that can be sustained in the face of challenge.

This chapter explores the issues identified above by exploring four themes:

- understanding ethics, values and morality
- developing moral confidence
- how we are to live
- morality in schools.

Understanding ethics, values and morality

Ethics, values and morality are often used as interchangeable terms and, as long as the usage is consistent, there is probably no problem with this. However, without getting into a semantic cul-de-sac, there are technical definitions which can help us clarify and refine their usage in education. It might be helpful to see their relationship to spirituality in the model in Figure 3.1.

In this model, spirituality is the heart – the core – of our behaviour. It is the basis for all our choices and the primary source of consistency. From our most profound spiritual beliefs we derive our ethical principles. These are the broadly based general rules by which we decide to live our life. Such rules are usually derived from religious, philosophical or legal systems. However, such rules are usually generic, often historic and need to be interpreted to make sense in a particular context at a given time. This is the process of converting generic principles into personal values, which are significant, meaningful and relevant. It is these values that provide us with the precepts that we take into our daily lives. Nevertheless, such values are abstract and hypothetical and are tested on a daily basis by new, unforeseen situations. It is how we translate our values into daily practice that determines our morality. Morality is about how we actually behave – the concrete manifestations of our values, ethics and spirituality.

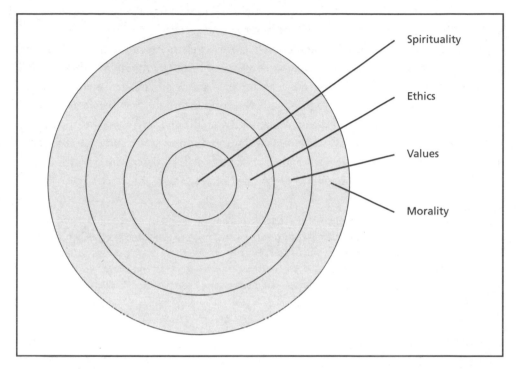

Figure 3.1 Relating ethics, values and morality to spirituality

For example, at the spiritual level a person may be committed to the integrity and sanctity of every human life. This is translated into an ethical framework which states that any form of violence against a person is wrong. Realistically, however, there are situations where this absolute may not be applicable, for example in self-defence, to protect a child or prevent a greater evil. The way in which we interpret broad ethical principles will define our personal values. The way that we apply our values on a practical, daily basis determines our morality. Thus, a person lives a life that avoids inflicting violence on another and will never support acts of violence in their name.

> We cannot expect to find in our society a single set of moral concepts ... Conceptual conflict is endemic in our situation because of the depth of our moral conflicts. Each of us therefore has to choose both with whom we wish to be morally bound and by what ends, rules, and virtues we wish to be guided. (MacIntyre, 1966, page 268)

It might be helpful to think of our values as a tree: spirituality is the tap root, the basis of the tree's existence and the primary source of its life. The other roots provide the ethical system that secures the tree in the ground and feeds it. The trunk represents the particular configuration of personal values. It bears the branches which interact with the world – the ability of a tree to survive a storm depends on the strength of the branches linked to the trunk in turn secured by the roots. The roots have to be embedded in the soil – which nourishes, sustains and secures.

In nature there is a constant interaction between all elements of the tree, as it is with leading a moral life. A moral crisis may force a time of healing and repair; a drought will force the tree to draw on its innermost resources – a new situation will compel us to return to first principles. Living a public life is a constant interaction between personal values and public morality. Personal authenticity, credibility and trust will be largely determined by the extent to which morals, values, ethics and spirituality are consistent across contexts and over time. Personal sustainability will be determined by the extent to which these elements are based on personal choice and consent.

> What this suggests, therefore, is the responsible but exciting possibility of rethinking morality for our own day, acknowledging our situation, its confusions and insights, while also recognising that we need order and balance in our lives. But today, perhaps for the first time, we shall struggle to achieve a morality that is self-imposed and consented to by our own reasons, though even that will not guarantee our compliance. (Holloway, 2004, page 32)

Holloway goes on to argue:

> Command moralities may exercise a nostalgic appeal in a time of confusion. A second look at them ought to discourage us from trying to replicate them today. Whatever other characteristics the emerging morality must have, it must be characterised by the principle of consent. (ibid., page 33)

Developing moral confidence

Moral education raises worries that were explored in Chapter 1: it is easy to transmit information in a hierarchical, authoritarian way – it is much more difficult to secure authentic engagement and consent. This implies the development of personal understanding (see Chapter 4) and commitment, so that individuals develop the personal confidence to act in an appropriate way. Moral confidence is about having the ability to make the right choice, to resist peer pressure, to speak out and to accept the consequences of an unpopular action. Moral confidence is found in the whistleblower, the person who resigns as a matter of conscience, the individual who accepts responsibility when it would be easy to walk away.

Such behaviours cannot be achieved as the result of rote learning or communal acquiescence – they have to be based in reason. Law (2006) proposes the essential components of an approach to moral education based in reason:

Children should be encouraged to scrutinize their own beliefs and explore other points of view. While not wanting to be overly prescriptive, I would suggest that skills to be cultivated should at least include the ability to:

- reveal and question underlying assumptions,

- figure out the perhaps unforeseen consequences of a moral decision or point of view,

- spot and diagnose faulty reasoning,

- weigh up evidence fairly and impartially,

- make a point clearly and concisely,

- take turns in a debate, and listen attentively without interrupting,

- argue without personalizing a dispute,

- look at issues from the point of view of others, and

- question the appropriateness of, or the appropriateness of acting on, one's own feelings.

Acquiring these skills involves developing, not just a level of intellectual maturity, but a fair degree of emotional maturity too. (page 35)

This is a very sophisticated list of intellectual skills – often sadly lacking in the world's great debating chambers and corridors of power. Historical approaches to moral development have argued that, because children cannot think in this way, morality has to be imposed. Law goes on to argue:

To sum up: there's good evidence that children, even fairly young children, can think philosophically. And, while more research needs to be done, there's a growing body of evidence that it's good for them academically, socially and emotionally The kinds of skills such philosophy programmes foster are, surely, just the sort of skills we need new citizens to develop. (page 39)

Pritchard (1996) agrees with this point and goes on to argue:

The *Looking for Meaning* program's contribution to the moral education of children builds on the already rather well-developed rational and moral abilities of its readers. It is important to keep this in mind for two reasons. First, it reinforces the educational point that children ... should not be regarded as 'empty vessels' into whom moral values must be poured (a form of moral indoctrination). They are active inquirers, ready and willing to offer their own rendering of the issues at hand. Second, a moral point that follows from the first, to fail to respect these capacities in children is to fail to respect children as the moral agents they are. (page 52)

A potentially useful way of developing an approach to developing moral confidence is to distinguish between normative and analytic approaches to morality. We are all probably most familiar with normative approaches – we behave in a certain way because we should. The origins of normative statements are found in alternative models of power. A person behaves in a certain way because they believe that is what is required by God, parents or the law – or even schools. Normative approaches to morality are usually based on belief, acceptance and, often, the fear of sanctions. Historically, the moral development of young people was seen as a process of induction into a code of behaviour, which usually involved descriptions of the desired way of behaving accompanied by illustrations of the sanctions that would accompany failure to observe these ways. Perhaps the most extreme examples of this are to be found in James Joyce's *Portrait of the Artist as a Young Man.*

Such approaches seem to work, most of us do not murder, steal or break the speed limit because there is a range of sanctions of varying degrees of severity and immediacy. However, morality that is based on obedience, compliance and the threat of sanction will always be fragile because it is based on external negative compulsion. Society has, largely, rejected such an approach.

> The main characteristic of our new, lightweight moral tradition will be the principle of consent. Just as obedience to the commands of authority, whether God, state or any other centre of power, was the dominant characteristic of ancient traditions, so, today, is the consent of our reason and emotion. Today, we expect to be persuaded by coherent argument and the consequential results of particular policies. (Holloway, pages 156–7)

Holloway's advocacy of consent as the basis for moral development has profound implications for the role of education in moral development:

> One of the most important balances to achieve in the new morality of consent would be between celebrating an allowable diversity in ethical approaches and refusing to accept the claim that no system is better than any other. … We have recognised that moral struggles are frequently between competing goods, rather than between a straight good and a straight evil But that does not mean that anything goes … (ibid., page 159)

This leads to an exploration of the analytic approach to moral development. In essence, this involves moving from obedience to consent, from conformity to understanding and, critically, the ability to make an informed choice.

If developing moral confidence is a matter of thinking rather than obeying, then there is a number of implications for how schools approach this complex topic:

1. School norms and culture are highly influential in determining, explicitly and implicitly, what constitutes appropriate moral behaviour.

2. Discussions about behaviour need to apply the principles set out by Stephen Law (above). Very often learning about morality in the classroom is not paralleled in the corridor, where power rather than reason often rules.

3. The development of moral confidence requires the explicit development of cognitive and emotional skills – in the same way that an athlete needs basic fitness training as well as technical skills.

4. Moral understanding, and so confidence, is significantly determined by social interaction – we are influenced through observing the moral choices of others. Wittgenstein (1958) quotes St Augustine describing the development of language:

> When they [my elders] named some object, and accordingly moved towards something, I saw this and I grasped that the thing was called by the sound they uttered when they meant to point it out. Their intention was shewn by their bodily movements ... Thus, as I heard words repeatedly used in their proper places in various sentences, I gradually learnt to understand what objects they signified ... (page 2)

A very similar process occurs with the development of moral behaviour. We observe others modelling behaviour and replicate that behaviour.

5. One of the principal factors that determine the nature of a family, school, community or any organization is the extent to which there is an agreed and explicit set of rules, code of conduct or agreed values. The process of developing such codes is often as important as the actual content. Agreeing and securing the consent to a moral code is, of itself, a moral act. The conversations, dialogue, negotiation and consensus seeking involved in the process offer the classic choice of 'do as I say' or 'do as I do'.

6. The growth of moral confidence is significantly enhanced through challenge, testing and comparison. Exposure to alternative perspectives, exploring the applicability of principles in varying contexts and debating underlying assumptions are all part of the process of developing and sustaining moral confidence.

Moral confidence is best understood by reference to:

- a sense of personal authenticity;
- an acceptance of personal responsibility – a recognition of personal autonomy;
- the ability to engage with others;
- a recognition of the continuing need to learn and develop as a moral being.

How are we to live?

The title of this section is taken from Singer's (1997) study, which is subtitled 'ethics in an age of self-interest'. He argues that the whole point of ethical and moral development is to:

> … reinstate the idea of living and ethical life as a realistic and viable alternative to the present dominance of materialist self-interest. If, over the next decade, a critical mass of people with new priorities were to emerge, and if these people were seen to do well, in every sense of the term – if they find joy and fulfillment in their lives – then the ethical attitude will spread, and the conflict between ethics and self-interest will have been shown to be overcome, not by abstract reasoning alone, but by adopting the ethical life as a practical way of living, and showing that it works, psychologically, socially and ecologically. (page 279)

This, of course, begs the question as to what constitutes an ethical life – how do we know if we are living a good life? Indeed, how do we define good?

There are numerous permutations of what appear to be remarkably consistent possibilities and interjections as to how we should behave. These seem to endure across time and are found, with a range of cultural nuances, in most societies. At the risk of parody, it seems that 'don't kill', 'don't steal' and 'be kind' cover most ethical formulations and moral prescriptions. The major debates of the philosophers and theologians seem to focus on the interpretation and application of these principles. Is assassinating a genocidal dictator murder? Is stealing to feed a starving baby theft? Do I have to be kind to everybody all the time?

The world's religions help us to answer these questions by providing rules – their response is quintessentially normative. Ethical philosophers have long sought to find a minimalist formulation that will inform debate and so the emergence of a rational approach to ethics. From this perspective it may be more helpful to consider the questions that we need to engage with rather than focus on the rote learning of answers provided by others and enforced through power and sanctions. This enables us to focus on the notion that, in a liberal democracy, the aim of moral education should be informed consent rather than unthinking compliance. Informed consent moves us from mindless acquiescence to conscious choices and, perhaps more importantly, the ability to respond to new situations. Grayling (2002) makes the case for a liberal education thus:

> … [it] opens the possibility for us to live more reflectively and knowledgeably, especially about the nature and variety of human experience. That, in turn, increases our capacity for understanding others better, so that we can treat them with respect and sympathy, however different their outlook on life. (page 9)

... for the aim of liberal education is to help people continue learning all their lives long, and to think, and to question. New and challenging moral dilemmas are always likely to arise, so we need to try to make ourselves the kind of people who can respond thoughtfully. (pages 9–10)

The answer to Singer's question: 'How are we to live?' might thus be found in the notion that we apply the principles of liberal rationality to a range of dilemmas and seek to understand the implications of our actions. Understanding the implications of any action can be seen as a fundamental criterion of moral understanding, confidence and maturity. It is often argued that children are not always able to understand the implications of their actions – hence the concept of the age of criminal responsibility. Most societies argue that moral awareness is a product of maturity. However, this is almost always in the context of normative ethics – when children are told how to behave rather than helped to understand the significance of moral choices. For Dawkins (2006) moral behaviour is essentially biological in origin.

But what about the wrenching compassion we feel when we see an orphaned child weeping, an old widow in despair from loneliness, or an animal whimpering in pain? What gives us the powerful urge to send an anonymous gift of money or clothes to tsunami victims on the other side of the world whom we shall never meet, and who are highly unlikely to return the favour? Where does the Good Samaritan in us come from? (page 215)

In what might be interpreted as a liberating and life-enhancing possibility, he argues that moral behaviour is actually a product of our evolution:

The 'mistake' or 'by-product' idea, which I am espousing, works like this. Natural selection, in ancestral times when we lived in small and stable bands like baboons, programmed into our brains altruistic urges, alongside sexual urges, hunger urges, xenophobic urges and so on ...

I am suggesting that the same is true of the urge to kindness – to altruism, to generosity, to empathy, to pity. In ancestral times, we had the opportunity to be altruistic only towards close kin and potential reciprocators. Nowadays that restriction is no longer there, but the rule of thumb persists. Why would it not? (ibid., page 221)

Moral education is thus a process of helping people understand their social relationships and their own interests within those relationships. The problem is, of course, that humanity is not rational – or, more accurately, that humanity has never been educated to be rational. We behave inappropriately because we have not been given the skills and strategies to think about moral issues.

Once the skills and strategies are in place then it becomes possible to explore the status, significance, relevance and, crucially, the interpretation of the qualities, behaviours, codes and formulations that are seen as the components of moral behaviour. For most readers the Ten Commandments would be the most obvious and best-known example of a set of moral precepts designed to inform how we live our lives. Comte-Sponville (1996, pages vii–viii) identifies what he calls 'the great virtues':

1. Politeness
2. Fidelity
3. Prudence
4. Temperance
5. Courage
6. Justice
7. Generosity
8. Compassion
9. Mercy
10. Gratitude
11. Humility
12. Simplicity
13. Tolerance
14. Purity
15. Gentleness
16. Good Faith
17. Humour
18. Love

There seems little doubt that if a person displaying all of these virtues could be found we would regard them as a paragon – and probably be deeply suspicious of them. Each of the virtues is an ideal that we have to seek to understand and then act on as best we can:

> Every virtue is a summit between two vices, a crest between two chasms: hence courage stands between cowardice and temerity, dignity between servility and selfishness, gentleness between anger and apathy, and so on. But who can dwell on the high summits all the time? To think about the virtues is to take measure of the distance separating us from them. To think about their excellence is to think about our own inadequacies or wretchedness. (Comte-Sponville, 1996, page 5)

How we behave is determined by a complex web of interconnecting variables – the relative significance of each component will vary according to context and time. What remains constant is that all moral behaviour has to be based on choice and consent if it is to be meaningful, authentic and significant.

Morality in schools

A child's moral development will be in response to a wide range of factors, of which the most important will probably be the behaviour and expectations of his or her family and the community in which he or she lives. The school sits uneasily in relation to these two – it is potentially a highly significant influence but only to the extent that reflects a social consensus and builds on norms and expectations experienced in the family and community. Where such norms are absent, then the school has a vital role in building moral confidence. Where there are tensions and contradictions between the school and its environment, the school will always be at a disadvantage if it is just an agency for the articulation and enforcement of arcane rules and resolutions.

A more positive and appropriate approach, building on the points made earlier in this chapter, might be to see the school as a moral community working through consent and reason. If the school is thought of as a learning community then, according to Sergiovanni (1992), the following issues have to be explored:

- How the learning community will be defined.
- What the relationships will be among parents, students, teachers, and administrators if the school is to become a community.
- What shared values, purposes, and commitments bond the community.
- How parents, teachers, administrators, and students will work together to embody these values.
- What kinds of obligations to the community members should have and how these will be enforced. (page 46)

Each of these concerns is a moral issue and the exploration of responses to them is essentially, in Sergiovanni's terms, about the creation of a virtuous school. He introduces the idea of a covenant that is:

> … able to provide the kind of morally based contractual relationship that can bond people together. Bonding relationships respond to the reality that emotion, values, and membership connections are important human impulses. They also acknowledge the aspect of human nature that places other interests before self-interest. Finally, they give needed meaning and significance to our lives. These inclinations join covenant and virtue. It is difficult to talk about school covenants without also concerning oneself with what comprises the virtuous school. (ibid., page 102)

The creation of such a covenant is at least as significant as its content. In working to create a covenant, a social contract or a shared understanding of community leadership is a vital ingredient. One of the determining conditions of effective leadership is that it should be morally driven. It is therefore incumbent on all school leaders to:

- apply moral codes consistently;
- model appropriate behaviours;
- engage in dialogue to secure understanding and commitment;
- celebrate examples of appropriate behaviour;
- challenge examples of inappropriate behaviour;
- constantly monitor, review and evaluate the relevance and validity of moral codes.

Consider the following banal and rather obvious examples of the tensions inherent in making schools moral communities:

- A casually dressed teacher berating an 18-year-old student for his temerity in wearing trainers in school.
- Teachers ignoring one-way systems in school and the queuing system at lunchtime because they are 'very busy'.
- Teachers who are smokers punishing students caught smoking.

The issue in each case is the abuse of positional power which immediately denies the possibility of the school becoming a moral community. Organizations are quite comfortable with carefully differentiated notions of equity (for example the directors' dining room and the workers' canteen) but if schools are for students (rather than adults) then surely equity has to start with them? Schools are remarkably inconsistent when it comes to being moral communities. They publish aims, mission statements, and so on, which often do not refer to adults, yet students are not involved in the creation of these statements. Schools emphasize their commitment to students, yet in social terms it is often much better to be an adult. If a school's aims are seen as a set of promises, then the extent to which the school is a moral community, and has an authentic covenant, will be determined by the way in which these promises are kept.

Morality can never be a 'taught' subject; it has to be a lived, shared experience with a moral consensus developed through dialogue and reason involving all members of the community. The movement from compliance to consent; from passive acceptance to active engagement; from rote learning to understanding is all about the difference between schooling and educating.

4 Understanding deep and profound learning

A great potential danger in discussing the spiritual and moral development of young people is that we fail to see it as a learning process. It sometimes feels as if spiritual and moral learning is a process akin to osmosis, in other words learning by proximity or it's simply a matter of replicating the appropriate language and behaviours. The probably apocryphal story of the child singing the words of a hymn 'Gladly, the cross-eyed bear' rather than 'Gladly, the cross I'd bear' demonstrates the gap between simply repeating language and personal understanding.

Spiritual and moral development has to be seen as a learning process that involves intellectual activity. Most importantly it involves a movement away from shallow and superficial repetition into deep learning that is characterized by the growth of personal understanding. Perhaps the most concise and yet complete definition of deep learning is provided by Dewey (1933):

> We state emphatically that, upon its intellectual side education consist in the formation of wide-awake, careful, thorough habits of thinking. Of course intellectual learning includes the amassing and retention of information. But information is an undigested burden unless it is understood. It is knowledge only as its material is comprehended. And understanding, comprehension, means that the various parts of the information acquired are grasped in their relations to one another – a result that is attained only when acquisition is accompanied by constant reflection upon the meaning of what is studied. (pages 78–9)

Dewey emphasizes the essential components of deep learning as:

- differentiating information and knowledge;
- focusing on understanding;
- seeing reflection as the key process.

Dewey provides us with a model of deep learning that applies to almost every human activity – it is essentially the movement from knowing 'what?' to knowing 'how?' and 'why?' Much of our experience of schooling is centred on knowing 'what?':

> The result is knowledge that may not be inert; it can serve practical and cognitive needs and provide a basis for further learning. But it does not in any fundamental way alter our outlook on the world. It does not make us better people. Every once in a while, something does break through. We encounter a powerful idea or read a powerful book or hear a powerful piece of music that changes us, that radiates through our whole person. … Needless to say, such education would not be imposed on the learner. It would make contact with the deepest wellsprings of the learner's thought and feeling; natural processes would take it from there. (Leithwood et al., 2006, page 15)

Spiritual and moral development has to be about learning that 'radiates through our whole person' and is concerned with the 'deepest wellsprings'. Unfortunately, deep learning is a complex process for the teacher and the learner; it is difficult to codify and classify and so difficult to access. It is much easier to deliver content than to support the emergence of understanding. The ability to articulate, however accurately, the content of a code of conduct is no guarantee of appropriate behaviour. Memorizing a catechism is not an indicator of religious understanding, while reading a book on emotional intelligence is no indicator of personal or interpersonal effectiveness.

Defining learning

Before debating the nature of deep learning it is necessary to differentiate between the various usages of learning. Learning is a highly ambiguous and contested concept. Common usage would include the following definitions:

1. A qualitative increase in information.
2. Learning as memorizing.
3. Learning as developing skills and techniques.
4. Learning as creating understanding, seeing relationships and being aware of the cognitive processes involved.
5. Learning as creating new realities, developing wisdom and re-creating knowledge.

Usages 1, 2 and 3 may be characterized as shallow learning that can be defined as managing and memorizing information. The fourth and fifth categories apply to deep and profound leaning in that knowledge is created and understood through the use of higher-order cognitive skills, for example analysis, synthesis and application. Profound learning is the extension of deep learning so that it becomes personal to the learner.

Spiritual and moral development has to be about deep and profound learning or it will become the unthinking recitation of a catechism, a sort of philosophical or theological 'trivial pursuit'.

The broad differences between shallow, deep and profound learning are presented in the model in Figure 4.1.

	Shallow What?	Deep How?	Profound Why?
Means	Memorization	Reflection	Intuition
Outcomes	Information	Knowledge	Wisdom
Evidence	Replication	Understanding	Meaning
Motivation	Extrinsic	Intrinsic	Moral
Attitudes	Compliance	Interpretation	Challenge
Relationships	Dependence	Independence	Interdependence
	(Single loop)	(Double loop)	(Triple loop)

Figure 4.1 Modes of learning (West-Burnham and Coates, 2005, page 35)

The essential characteristics of each mode of learning may be summarized as follows:

Shallow learning is focused on the memorization and replication of information; uncritical acceptance of facts; rote learning; seeing information as unrelated and isolated themes; learners are passive; emphasis on coverage of content; assessment is summative; content is quickly forgotten. It is controlled by the teacher with the learner compliant and dependent.

It is this compliance and dependence that inhibits moral and spiritual development – in the worst-case scenario it results in the 'I'm only obeying orders' syndrome – unthinking and unquestioning acquiescence. Shallow learning does have a place in moral and spiritual growth in creating the language and laying the foundations of information that may enable deep and profound learning to take place.

Deep learning is focused on the creation of knowledge through the demonstration of understanding; the analysis and synthesis of facts to create conceptual models and frameworks; integrating prior learning and cross-referencing to other themes and subjects; learning is active and based in relationships; emphasis on depth; assessment is formative and negotiated; content is remembered and codified. Deep learning is controlled by the learner, who understands the learning process with the teacher as facilitator, mentor and co-constructor of knowledge.

Profound learning: the situation where knowledge becomes wisdom, in other words, intuitive and fundamental to the identity of the person; the capacity to create new meaning in changing situations and contexts; developing a holistic awareness of the relationship between themes, subjects, principles and practice; assessment is through personal authenticity and integrity. The teacher becomes the guide, inspiration, friend and counsellor, the *anam cara*.

Profound learning has many manifestations, from learning to talk in childhood to the artistry of the concert pianist; from the skills and compassion of the nurse to the great scientific discovery; from the skill of the joiner to the creativity of the painter.

Shallow learning is playing the notes; deep learning creates the melody; profound learning enables the great performance. Shallow learning gives access to vocabulary and the rules of grammar; deep learning allows conversations; profound learning enables engagement with poetry, ideas and thinking. Profound learning is the characteristic of the Formula One motor racing driver, the mentor, the highly successful learner and athlete. Profound learning moves us from religious observance to spirituality.

Engaging with deep and profound learning

The movement from shallow to deep and profound learning can be best characterized as the growth of personal understanding, of ownership and the movement away from dependency. As a child learns to read and write he or she gradually grows in confidence and autonomy – his or her increasing understanding is manifested in personal autonomy. Spiritual and moral development is potentially more challenging as it requires engagement with complex and abstract theories, models and concepts. Just as writing moves from mechanical replication to self-directed creativity, so we need to find a parallel process for spiritual and moral learning.

Success in academic terms is often measured in terms of comfort and ease with abstract concepts. Indeed the process of developing mastery in any given subject can be directly related to fluency in that subject's specialist language. Such a language is usually expressed in terms of concepts, for example from being able to recite the causes of the First World War to understanding the concept of causality.

Dealing with abstract concepts is one of the most challenging components of learning and teaching. Thus, in mathematics I might understand the protocols of subtraction but the concept of negative numbers is totally baffling. Hayward and Jones (2001, page 17) offer a range of reasons why working with concepts is difficult:

- Concepts are abstract – they cannot be pointed to.

- Concepts have 'fuzzy boundaries' – they are vague and contested.
- Concepts are irrelevant – they do not have concrete manifestations.
- Concepts use complex and arcane language – they are jargon.
- Conceptual issues have no right answers – they involve value judgements.
- Concepts do not always relate to content – there are no facts.
- Concepts are personal – they can involve matters of belief and faith which are private.

Moving from shallow to deep and profound learning in the context of spiritual and moral development is essentially the process of responding to these challenges. Hayward and Jones (2001) suggest a way forward:

> The learning outcomes of lessons involving conceptual subjects cannot be based solely on the factual content, as this does not exist in many instances. The outcomes may involve such things as raising awareness, exploring different opinions, encouraging critical thinking, working with others, expressing opinions etc. These outcomes are almost impossible to achieve if the subject is learnt passively. If would seem that a more active model of teaching is the only way such outcomes could be achieved. (pages 17–18)

The second section of this book offers a wide portfolio of strategies to support the movement to active learning but in broad terms these strategies might be summarized as follows:

- Moving from the concrete to the abstract, from personal experience to generic principles.
- Working through scenarios, hypothetical situations and case studies.
- Providing strategies and techniques to support prioritization, classification and demonstrate relationships.
- Building shared vocabulary and creating opportunities for dialogue and conversation.
- Working through problem-solving techniques based on appropriate challenges.
- Systematic and regular review of what has been learned, how it has been learned and the implications for future learning.

At the heart of moral and spiritual development is the process of internalization – the movement from generic, public information to specific, personal knowledge, in other words becoming a person.

> To become conscious in some degree of the eternally Real, through one of its humanly experienceable manifestations, is in that degree to be liberated from the anxious, grasping ego, and freed to love one's neighbour, who is anyone and everyone. We see something of the extraordinary possibilities of our own nature. (Hick, 1999, page 254)

Guignon (2004) provides an alternative perspective, focusing on the social rather than the transcendental:

> (1) knowing what you believe and feel and (2) honestly expressing those beliefs and feelings in what you do. For this purpose, it is less important *what* you believe and feel than *how* deep those feelings and beliefs are. The modern picture of the ideal person is a picture of an independent, self-directed individual whose actions clearly manifest what he or she really is. It is an image of a focused, effective agent interacting with others and participating in public affairs with a degree of clarity, courage and integrity normally lacking in inauthentic individuals. (page 150)

In both cases such a stage of development has to be rooted in the deep and profound.

There is not necessarily a causal relationship from shallow to deep and on to profound. There are many examples of people who go directly to deep and profound – some never pass shallow.

Of course we have to be very careful when talking of genius, prodigies and savants. They are, by definition, exceptional. Thus, the young Mozart (and even more remarkably the young Mendelssohn) displayed both creative genius *and* technical mastery – notably orchestration. There are numerous examples of child prodigies in chess, music and mathematics. Interestingly there are fewer examples in the literary domains. This may reflect cultural patterns or different aspects of cognitive development. Precocious ability seems to be more likely in those disciplines using symbolic notation.

Our society prizes genius or exceptional ability but often fails to honour less dramatic examples of insight and understanding. For example, the cases of children who are carers for ill parents, who often display remarkable levels of empathy, altruism and compassion. Or the chronically ill children who challenge us with their dignity, grace and courage. It is a sad reflection of a society that values schooling above educating, that we celebrate 17 GCSEs at A* but fail to recognize personal authenticity.

Equally, deep and profound are not homogeneous for all aspects of learning – thus, the same person may be shallow with regard to information communication technology (ICT), deep in their understanding of learning and teaching and profound in their interpersonal relationships.

It is possible to be shallow, deep or profound in each of Gardner's multiple intelligences. The chess grand master may lack interpersonal intelligence; the person with high linguistic intelligence may lack spatial and kinaesthetic abilities. Pivotal to deep learning and the foundation of profound learning is understanding:

> An individual understands a concept, skill, theory, or domain of knowledge to the extent that he or she can apply it.

> This formulation entails an acid test for understanding: posing to students a topic or theme or demonstration that they have never before encountered, and determining what sense they can make of those phenomena. An individual who possesses relevant understanding will be able to draw on appropriate concepts.
>
> (Gardner, 1999, page 119)

Perkins (1998, page 77) develops a definition of the indicators of deep learning that can be equally applied to profound learning – it is essentially a matter of degree, of depth, confidence and sophistication:

- Explanation: the ability to create and share meaning.
- Classification: the ability to analyse and codify.
- Exemplification: the capacity to describe, model and illustrate.
- Transfer: the ability to see and make connection between topics and themes.
- Justification: a tendency to ask 'why?', 'how?' and 'what if?' questions.
- Comparison: the ability to contrast and identify common characteristics.
- Contextualization: the ability to recognize relationships and differences.
- Generalization: the ability to formulate hypotheses and patterns.
- Action: the ability to translate theory into practice.
- Metacognition: self-awareness and self-direction.

We have added the last two to reinforce our definition of deep and profound learning. Learning for understanding enables us to explore our potential as human beings:

> By learning the use and the meaning of words as children we acquire more than a communication tool. We also acquire a taxonomy, a way of categorizing the virtual infinity of things, events, and impressions that is the world, and thus of making our world stable and manageable. ... By coming into possession of this linguistic treasure trove, we come into possession of the knowledge and wisdom of generations. (Goldberg, 2005, page 91)

In the context of moral and spiritual development, Perkins' list can be elaborated and extended to exemplify the criteria for deep and profound learning:

- Explanation: the ability to demonstrate understanding by elucidating and describing why something is valued or significant.
- Classification: the ability to codify, to demonstrate relationships and indicate relative significance and status, in other words to prioritize moral imperatives.
- Exemplification: the capacity to illustrate and illuminate so as to make meaning clear and distinct, for example the development of stories and parables.

- Transfer: the ability to link concepts or ideas across contexts, for example moving from personal experience to universal principles.

- Justification: being able to demonstrate the rationale behind a belief or precept; to argue for a particular stance.

- Comparison: the ability to identify similarities and differences, for example the comparative study of religions and philosophies.

- Contextualization: the ability to demonstrate the implications and impact of context, for example the significance of culture on belief.

- Generalization: the ability to extrapolate principles and roles from personal experience.

- Action: the confidence to act on the basis of personal understanding and to make consistent and valid choices.

- Metacognition: understanding and awareness of the learning process and the ability to select the most appropriate effective learning strategies, for example the relationship between experience and reflection.

Supporting the deep and profound learner

In his model of 'powerful learning' (that has many of the characteristics of deep learning) B]randt (1998) argues that there are a range of conditions necessary for learning to take place:

In general, we can say that people learn well under the following conditions:

What They Learn

1. What they learn is personally meaningful.

2. What they learn is challenging and they accept the challenge.

3. What they learn is appropriate for their developmental level.

How They Learn

4. They can learn their own way, have choices, and feel in control.

5. They use what they already know as they construct new knowledge.

6. They have opportunities for social interaction.

7. They get helpful feedback.

8. They acquire and use strategies.

Where They Learn

9. They experience a positive emotional climate.

10. The environment supports the intended learning.

(page 12)

These general principles can be translated into a number of specific strategies:

- A clear understanding of learning styles, aptitudes, dispositions and motivation supported by regular review and the development of strategies to enhance and sustain personal learning effectiveness.

- Access to a portfolio of cognitive strategies – analysis, synthesis, causality and cognitive skills, for example memorizing.

- Teaching that is based on challenge (possibly using the Csikszentmihalyi model of flow), problem solving and relevant decision making.

- Teachers who work using constructivist approaches; the widespread use of coaching and mentoring, and the facilitation of small group and team-based strategies.

- The development of sophisticated interpersonal relationships and high emphasis on the social dimensions of learning. The development of emotional literacy across the school.

- The use of personalized learning pathways with negotiated learning outcomes and assessment for learning strategies to ensure relevance and potential application. The curriculum as a personal construct.

- A focus on the 'whole' learner, recognizing the role of the family and community in supporting access to effective learning.

- Systematic review and reflection.

On the basis of these propositions it is possible to identify the characteristics of the learner and teacher engaged in deep and profound learning:

> The effective learner knows how she learns and has a disposition to do so. She can identify, on her own, and/or with others, a problem, analyse its components and then organise herself to solve it.

> She continuously questions herself and others as to whether she is employing the best methods. She can explain the processes of her learning and its outcomes to her peers and others. She is able to organise information and, through understanding, convert it into knowledge. She is sensitive to her personal portfolio of intelligences and continually reviews her development as a learner. She knows when it is best to work alone, when with a mentor and when in a team, and knows how to contribute to and gain from teamwork. She sustains a sharp curiosity and takes infinite pains in all she does. She has the resilience to persevere when learning is difficult.

Above all, she has that security in self, built through a wide and deep set of relationships and through her own feelings of worth fostered in part by others, to be at ease with doubt, and to welcome questioning and probing of all aspects of her knowledge. She has a joy in her learning and in sharing the outcomes of that learning with others. She delights in enabling the learning of others. (Adapted from West-Burnham and Coates, 2005, page 38)

The effective teacher has a deep understanding of the neurological, cognitive, emotional and social aspects of learning. She balances this knowledge with the ability to access subject information and the strategies to convert it into personal knowledge.

She works through challenges, posing problems and setting questions ensuring that they are appropriate to the individual learner and that the learner has the skills to respond to them. She creates a sense of emotional security by building trust and confidence and working in an interdependent manner. She has a deep respect for the identity and integrity of every learner.

The effective teacher works primarily as a facilitator and mentor. She is skilled in negotiating learning strategies, understanding the learner's motivation and has a passionate belief in the potential of every learner. She recognizes, reinforces and celebrates achievement and ensures that there are abundant opportunities for the learner to experience valid and appropriate success. She is highly sensitive to the student's social context.

Above all, she models learning, reviewing her own practice with her mentor, deepening her understanding of the learning process and engaging in networks with other teachers.

In Steiner's memorable words:

… to teach, to teach well, is to be accomplice to transcendent possibility. Woken, that exasperating child in the back row may write the lines, may conjecture the theorem that will busy centuries.

No mechanical means, however expeditious, no materialism, however triumphant, can eradicate the daybreak we experience when we have understood … (2003, page 184)

In summary, deep and profound learning is the result of:

- Seeing learning as a process rather than an outcome.
- Developing a cognitive 'toolkit' – a repertoire of learning strategies and techniques.
- Ensuring that mentoring is a basic component of all learning activities.
- Providing opportunities to demonstrate understanding through formative and negotiated assessment.
- Focusing on learning through challenge.

Deep and profound learning are the *sine qua non* of moral and spiritual development. If we are to be confident that all children and young people are able to access the possibilities of personal growth and realize their potential as human beings, then we have to recognize the centrality of learning. It is not enough to hope that moral and spiritual capacity will be developed by benevolent interactions or rigorous transmission of information.

Central to moral and spiritual growth is a significant relationship that guides, supports, challenges and affirms. Crucially this relationship is rooted in dialogue and in the teacher as a model:

> What is missing from the world is a sense of direction, because we are overwhelmed by the conflicts which surround us, as though we are marching through a jungle which never ends. I should like some of us to start conversations to dispel that darkness, using them to create equality, to give ourselves courage, to open ourselves to strangers, and most practically, to remake our working world, so that we are no longer isolated by our jargon or our professional boredom. (Zeldin, 1998, page 97)

Deep and profound learning involves the shared creation of understanding – the basis for shared meaning and informed action. It is the basis of all significant human activity:

> It is the obligation of any society in which we would choose to live to maintain the openness and to facilitate the routes to new insights and new understandings. We oppose those psychological and educational approaches that threaten that openness or presume to deny its importance and even its existence. (Gardner, 2006a, page 212)

5 The school as a spiritual and moral community

Engagement with a community is essential to spiritual and moral development. As was demonstrated in Chapter 2, community is one of the most powerful vehicles for developing spiritual understanding. Apart from hermits and anchorites, most faiths and philosophies find their most powerful expression through community. Shared living, working, recreation and worship are seen as crucial to the development of senses of identity – both personal and collective. Equally, it is only through social interaction that we learn to be moral; indeed it could be argued that morality is the basis of social interaction. Morality remains an abstract ethical theory unless we apply it and it is in the application that we develop moral understanding and so learn to behave in a moral way.

This chapter argues for a change in the approach found in many schools, in other words moving away from the school as an effective organization to the school as a community.

Much of the emphasis in school improvement over the past 25 years has been on making schools work better as organizations, and issues of shared values and morality have been central to this. There does appear to be a very high correlation between academic and educational success and the efficacy of the school as an organization. However, if we are to move from incremental improvement in schooling to a focus on education and learning (as outlined in Chapters 2 and 5) then it is necessary to begin to think of the school as a community.

The movement from organization to community is more than just a matter of semantics. Organizations tend to have one specific function (in other words they are monotechnic), they employ people who are paid to carry out specific roles within an organizational structure. Organizations tend to have roles which are enforced through various types of accountability. Crucially, people's engagement in organizations is conditional: the '9 to 5' syndrome. Organizations often work through power and control rather than consent. Perhaps the quickest way to distinguish an organization from a community is to argue that communities have 'soul'; organizations can be communities but they will need to rethink what they perceive to be significant:

> Love is largely absent in the modern corporation. Most managers would never use the word in any context more profound than their feelings about food, films, or games. They shy away from love's deeper meaning, fearing both its power and its risks. (Bolman and Deal, 1995, page 104)

> The gift of significance lets people find meaning in work, faith in themselves, confidence in the value of their lives, and hope for the future. Reason and technology often divert our attention from the everyday existential pillars that support our sense of significance. (ibid., page 113)

There is abundant evidence that living in an effective and authentic community enhances every dimension of our lives. We are healthier, happier, live longer and are less likely to be ill, to be involved in crime or the victim of crime if we live in a community.

Community is a 'hooray' word – everybody approves of it. There are many ways of defining what a community is. One of the most powerful and evocative is Archbishop Desmond Tutu's development of the Southern African concept of *ubuntu*. *Ubuntu* is one those words that is difficult to translate precisely – it can be rendered as 'I am because we are' or 'A person is a person through other people'. In both cases, the emphasis is on personal identity being the product of social interaction:

> *Ubuntu* refers to the person who is welcoming, who is hospitable, who is warm and generous, who is affirming of others, who does not feel threatened that others are able and good for [this person] has a proper self-assurance that comes from knowing they belong in a greater whole, and know that they are diminished when another is humiliated, is diminished, is tortured, is oppressed, is treated as if they were less than who they are. (Battle, 1997, page 45)

Ubuntu has significant moral and spiritual implications:

> Consequently injustice, racism, exploitation, oppression are to be opposed not as a political task but as a response to a religious, a spiritual imperative. (ibid., page 48)

Although it lacks the emotional power and cultural significance of *ubuntu*, the closest Western concept is social capital. According to Martin (2005):

... social capital consists of the social networks within community or society, together with the shared norms, values and understandings that facilitate cooperation within or among groups. Social capital arises from the networks of personal relationships between friends, neighbours and colleagues, and it encompasses such things as neighbourliness, community spirit, social cohesion, citizenship and trust. (page 87)

Social capital is what turns a village, a neighbourhood, an organization or a school into a community. In essence, social capital creates shared meaning and purpose through which individuals realize their full humanity. Although the term capital has financial implications, in this context it would be more helpful to see it in terms of potential and capacity. High social capital enhances both the community and the individual; low social capital diminishes both. If schools are to develop as communities, let alone as spiritual and moral communities, then one of the key tests of leaders, and all members of the school community, is the need to work to consciously address the development of the key variables that influence the level of social capital. Figure 5.1 illustrates the components of social capital.

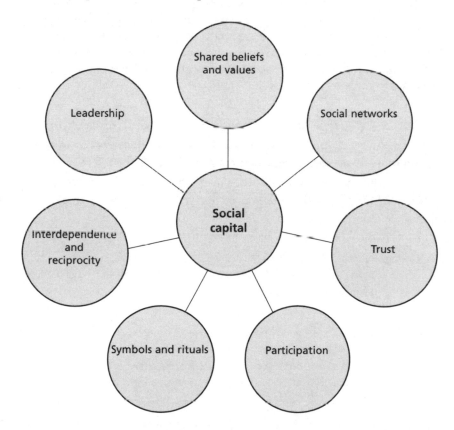

Figure 5.1 The components of social capital (adapted from West-Burnham et al., 2007, page 32)

Any diagram will convey an artificial sense of balance and integration. No community will have all these factors in place all of the time – each will ebb and flow and there will be a dynamic interaction between them – if a community is characterized by interdependence, then so are factors that make it a community. It is important to bear this in mind as each of these variables is explored in detail.

Shared beliefs and values

Successful communities achieve a high degree of homogeneity through agreement on the core beliefs and values that inform collective and individual choices and behaviour. This is neither to argue for a bland uniformity nor to deny the importance of personal belief and individual conscience. It is recognition that a community requires consistency, what Senge (1990) calls 'alignment':

> … a commonality of direction emerges, and individuals' energies harmonize. There is less wasted energy. In fact, a resonance or synergy develops, like the 'coherent' light of a laser rather than the incoherent and scattered light of a light bulb. There is commonality of purpose, a shared vision, and understanding of how to complement one another's efforts. Individuals do not sacrifice their personal interests to the larger team vision: rather the shared vision becomes an extension of their personal visions. (pages 234–5)

This last point is vital: the community harnesses and engages with individual perceptions – the beliefs and values emerge through a complex process of dialogue and negotiation. One of the most significant characteristics of the effective community is that it allows consensus to emerge rather than imposing and reinforcing it through organizational power. It is the function of leadership to facilitate emergence of this shared understanding:

> A binding and solemn agreement needs to emerge that represents a value system for living together and that provides the basis for decisions and actions. This binding and solemn agreement represents the school's covenant.

> When both vision and covenant are present, teachers and students respond with increased motivation and commitment and their performance is beyond expectations. The affirming of values that accompanies purposing is a motivational force far more powerful than the bureaucratic and psychological transactions that characterize leadership by bartering and building. (Sergiovanni, 1995, pages 132–3)

Sergiovanni here reinforces the movement from organization to community – consensus and commitment enhance both community and performance. Securing alignment is hard work, it is about building a shared language, agreeing norms and expectations and ensuring that the beliefs and values are not static but are being constantly revisited and revised.

For a school to grow as a spiritual and moral community it has to:

- be explicit about its commitment to moral and spiritual development;
- embed that commitment in its policies, procedures and roles;
- engage in meaningful conversations to ensure that all members of the community know, share, understand and act on agreed principles;
- regularly audit the impact of the above strategies.

Most importantly, the beliefs and values have to be expressed through all the other variables that contribute to social capital.

Social networks

Communities are about relationships, they constitute the most important expression of the community's beliefs and values. It is through relationships that many members of a school community will have their most direct experience of the possibilities for spiritual and moral growth. Organizations are often characterized by vertical communication (top down and/or bottom up); communities are characterized by lateral communication through multiple, complex and constantly developing networks. Rather like the way that the internet is supposed, in theory, to open and democratize communication, so, in effective communities, there are no gates and no gatekeepers. Networks in communities are rather like the neural networks of the brain; if they are not used they can wither and perhaps die. Neural networks become stronger and richer the more they are used. Any human being who is cognitively active has an astonishingly rich and complex pattern of neural networks. Exactly the same can be said of the way in which successful communities function.

Goleman (2006) argues for the importance of social intelligence as the basis for personal and collective effectiveness:

> The major functions of the social brain – interaction synchrony, the types of empathy, social cognition, interactions skills, and concern for others – all suggest strands of social intelligence. The evolutionary perspective challenges us to think afresh about the place of social intelligence in the taxonomy of human abilities – and recognize that 'intelligence' can include noncognitive abilities. (page 29)

Social capital is significantly influenced by the level of interpersonal skills available in a community. It is equally influenced by the opportunities to make use of those skills.

The strength of a spider's web, of a honeycomb in a beehive, is partly the result of the materials used but, more importantly of the way those materials are structured. Both are examples of strength through interdependence.

Effective networks contribute to spiritual and moral development because of their potential to enrich and enhance communication, foster creativity and secure engagement and commitment. A distributed network, with genuine parity between all the elements, then there is the possibility of form following function – the way a community works is a reflection of the principles on which it is designed. Open networks support the exchange of ideas, ensure access to knowledge, enable learning and reinforce the conversations about common purpose and shared beliefs.

For a school to reinforce its identity as a community and maximize the engagement of all its members it needs to:

• support the development of interpersonal skills and strategies;
• create and support open and distributed networks;
• provide space and time to enable networks to flourish;
• use networks to support moral and spiritual development.

Trust

Trust is pivotal to any relationship and community; it is also a vital manifestation of spiritual maturity and an important expression of a moral integrity. At its simplest, trust is a demonstration of intense spiritual understanding – at its most complex, it is the culmination of a sophisticated moral consensus.

According to O'Hara (2004) trust serves three functions in society:

• It is an integrative force, it helps build consensus.
• It enables people to work in a cooperative manner.
• It helps to reduce complexity by creating sophisticated relationships.

Trust is an elusive quality; it cannot be legislated for nor created by diktat. It is very fragile, takes years to create and is destroyed in a moment. Spiritual and moral growth both depend on trust, both require us to engage in fundamental issues exposing our innermost feeling and deepest beliefs. Any form of learning – from learning to swim to exploring our personal values in challenging situations – requires trust.

Bryk and Schneider (2002) identify three types of trust:

Organic Trust

Organic trust is predicated on the more or less unquestioning beliefs of individuals in the moral authority of a particular social institution, and characterizes closed, small-scale communities. In such social systems, individuals give their trust unconditionally; they believe in the rightness of the system, the moral character of its leadership, and all others who commit to the community. (page 16)

Contractual Trust

Here individuals and institutions stand in a much more constrained relation to one another. The basis for social exchange is primarily material and instrumental. Although personal friendships may arise over time through repeated interactions, social-psychological motivations remain modest, and the moral-ethical dimension is weak or nonexistent. A contract defines basic actions to be taken by the parties involved. (ibid., page 17)

Relational Trust

A complex web of social exchanges conditions the basic operations of schools. Embedded in the daily social routines of schools is an interrelated set of mutual dependencies among all key actors: students, teachers, principals and administrators and parents. (ibid., page 20)

Relational trust is made up of four elements, each of which relates back to the elements of spirituality and morality discussed in previous chapters:

1. Respect – genuineness and personal esteem.
2. Competence – people have the skills and qualities to carry out their professional duties.
3. Personal regard – engagement with, and recognition of, the whole person.
4. Integrity – consistency in working practices and evidence of an ethical foundation to work.

Relational trust thus is not something that can be achieved simply through some workshop, retreat, or form of sensitivity training, although all of these can be helpful. Rather, relational trust is forged in daily social exchanges. Through their actions, school participants articulate their sense of obligations toward others, and others in turn, come to discern the intentionality enacted here. Trust grows over time through exchanges where the expectations held for others are validated in action. (Bryk and Schneider, 2002, pages 136–7)

For Bryk and Schneider there is an absolute correlation between the level of relational trust and the academic performance of a school. Standards are raised because the school has become a community and focuses on broader educational issues; trust is a direct, public and tangible expression of moral principles and is only authentic and sustainable in the extent that it is rooted in a deep, spiritual perspective on the value of every human being.

Participation

Effective communities are essentially open, inviting all members to be full and active protagonists in determining the nature and development of their community. Participation in the life of the community has partial and moral implications, not least because of the argument that schools which function in a modern democracy should prepare their students for adult lives as citizens by allowing them to experience democracy rather than being told about it. The level of engagement in the life of a community is one of the best indicators of social capital and the extent to which the community is actually building capacity for the future.

Participation can take a wide variety of forms:

- standing for office;
- voting in representative elections;
- taking part in consultation procedures;
- accepting leadership responsibility;
- taking part in voluntary activities;
- engaging in charitable work.

What is important in developing schools as effective communities, and so sending an unequivocal moral message, is that everybody is included: teachers and all other staff, children and young people, their parents and members of the wider community.

Flutter and Rudduck (2004, pages 131–9) describe the advantages to schools of increasing student participation – although the benefits apply to all members of the community. This is summarized as follows:

- Full participation increases the potential for transforming the school.
- A more rounded view of the lives of members of the community emerges.
- The quality of learning and teaching can be improved through consultation.
- Participation increases autonomy and a sense of independence, and so develops personal responsibility.
- Individuals are able to share their sense of the reality in which they live and work.
- Participation empowers and enhances self-esteem.
- The school becomes more inclusive and democratic.
- Relationships are enhanced and there are opportunities to build trust.

Sizer and Sizer (1999) capture perfectly the relationship between the school as a community and spiritual and moral development:

Two words are of special importance. The moral order is *voluntary*; the adults and the students are partners in its creation and maintenance. … The relationship between the needs of the community and individual freedom is not something arbitrarily imposed; it is, rather, arrived at through explanation, exploration, and persuasion.

The second critical word is *equilibrium*. There has to be a unified (if not precisely uniform) culture. And there has to be room for the appropriate expression of individual convictions. These two are not necessarily in opposition, but they can be. … One is true to oneself. One is also true to one's communities. Each citizen must find his or her most defensible balance. School exists to help along that process. (pages 17–18)

Symbols and rituals

Communities need symbols and rituals to reinforce and celebrate their sense of collective identity. Military units celebrate their distinctiveness through their uniforms, badges, flags and arcane rituals (and so do schools). Football supporters wear their team's strip; there are T-shirts to declare to the world one's commitment to a range of causes. We need symbols as an expression of our engagement and commitment and to enhance a sense of pride and belonging.

Equally, we need rituals that allow us to have a sense of shared purpose and engagement. The most obvious examples are church services, school assemblies, military parades – most other rituals copy the essential features of these three: singing together, a formalized sequence of events and lots of shared congratulations on being members of the community. Eating and drinking together often plays a vital role in such rituals. A school prize-giving, a leavers' assembly, a shared silence at a memorial service, can all have a high emotional impact.

The importance of liturgy as an aid to spiritual engagement has long been recognized by all the faiths. Central to virtually every liturgical experience is music, covering the range from Gregorian chant at a High Mass to a military bugler sounding the 'Last Post', to a football crowd singing 'Abide with me'. Music can be used potently both as a means of both personal spiritual engagement and as the reinforcement of collective identity.

White (2000) provides a powerful example of how all of these factors can be brought together. She introduced 'reflection time' at the end of the day with her Year 4 class. The children sat in a circle around a candle with appropriate music playing. A stone was passed around and children spoke about issues that were significant in their day at school or in their lives:

This kind of approach focuses on enabling children to reflect on their learning and emotional experiences and feelings, as opposed to the more traditional approach, which places curriculum knowledge and content at its centre. ... they need to understand that they 'are exploring aspects of a universal quest, in which they are all engaged by virtue of being human'. ... During reflection time the children are gathered around a candle to help them focus, which in itself is quite a spiritual setting. There is a feeling of togetherness, which could be compared with the shared experience people describe when participating in celebration or prayer in a place of worship. The sense of global feeling is enhanced through music, which is often of 'spiritual type', and/or from different parts of the world. (page 8)

Linda White's approach serves multiple purposes but it is very clearly about developing reflection in the individual pupils in the class and developing a shared experience that fosters a sense of belonging and sharing. Personal spiritual growth is reinforced through shared symbols and rituals.

Interdependence and reciprocity

For Archbishop Desmond Tutu, interdependence is fundamental to any sense of community: 'We are made for a delicate network of interdependence' (cited in Battle, 1997, page 35).

Interdependence is an expression of our most profound humanity – it is how we become who we might be. Our potential as spiritual and moral beings is developed to the extent that we engage in interdependent and reciprocal relationships. Interdependency and reciprocity work at many levels. On the one hand they are about the give and take that characterizes the demands of family life. They also help us to understand friendship. Vernon (2005) follows Aristotle in identifying three types of friendship:

The first group are friends primarily because they are useful to each other ... they share goodwill because they get something out of the relationship. The second group are friends primarily because some pleasure is enjoyed by being together.

... the third group ... are people who love each other because of who they are in themselves. (page 3)

Each type of friendship represents a different level of interdependence and reciprocity. The same principle can be extrapolated into how a community works:

Most important for the issue at hand is the sociological fact that we find reinforcement for our moral inclinations and provide reinforcement to our fellow human beings, through the community. We are each other's keepers.

When the term *community* is used, the first notion that typically comes to mind is a place in which people know and care for one another – the kind of place in which people do not merely ask 'How are you?' as a formality but care about the answer. (Etzioni, 1995, page 31)

Effective communities work through 'common-cause', those aspects of life where we are enhanced, enriched and enabled by the extent to which we collaborate and care about each other – this is morality in action.

Interdependence and reciprocity enable us to give practical expression to our commitment to our community, but it also is a fertile field to enable spiritual growth through acts of compassion, charity and caring. The reciprocity between neighbours in watching over children, pets and plants is matched by the interdependence of children watching over each other in the playground.

If interdependence and reciprocity are absent, or disappear, the implications for a community are indeed stark. In his study of the collapse of the society on Easter Island, Diamond (2005) points to competition between the clans as one factor. The imperative to build bigger statues led to rivalry and competition which led in time to the exhaustion of all natural resources and the loss of a civilization – the replacement of interdependence and reciprocity marked the end of the island community.

The parallels between Easter Island and the whole modern world are chillingly obvious. … When the Easter Islanders got into difficulties, there was nowhere to which they could flee, nor to which they could turn for help; not shall we modern Earthlings have recourse elsewhere if our troubles increase. Those are the reasons why people see the collapse of Easter Island society as a metaphor, a worst-case scenario, for what may lie ahead of us in our own future. (Diamond, 2005, page 119)

Sacks (2000, page 286) cites phrases such as 'fellowship of sharing' and 'mutual regard' to illuminate what it is that actually makes a community work on a daily basis. In essence it is about caring, and that has profound moral and spiritual implications.

Leadership

Leadership is essential to the success of any social enterprise. There is a clear consensus that leadership has four key components:

- Developing and sustaining the moral integrity of the organization, school or community. Leadership is primarily concerned with making choices – every decision should reflect the moral basis of the community.
- Agreeing, confirming and sustaining the core purpose of the community – clarifying the focus

of all activities and ensuring that the community does not lose sight of its priorities.

• Developing and maintaining high-quality personal relationships and securing engagement and commitment by all members of the community.

• Ensuring that the community is able to engage with change, to secure improvement and, when necessary, to transform the community.

There are two important issues that emerge from this list. First, it has referred to leadership rather than a leader or leaders. There is increasing recognition that effective communities do not work through leaders with personal status but rather through leadership as a collective and shared capacity. This is about recognizing and respecting the potential of every member of the community to contribute to its effectiveness irrespective of age, experience or role. Second, leadership has to be focused on learning. For Hargreaves and Fink (2006) this means:

• Modelling and building strong and rewarding relationships by paying attention to the human side of school change

• Establishing a high-trust environment

• Developing and renewing a culture of learning and improvement at all levels through problem solving, inquiry, and intelligent, evidence-informed decision making

• Helping the school community develop and commit to a cohesive and compelling purpose that also prevents dissipation of initiative and effort

• Stimulating a culture of professional entrepreneurship in regard to innovations and ideas that benefit student learning

• Establishing and enforcing grown-up professional norms of civil argument and productive debate

• Ensuring that the voices of minority members of the culture always receive a proper hearing

• Doing all this within an unswerving commitment to improving learning and achievement for all students, especially those who are furthest behind. (pages 127–8)

Part 2
Practice

Introduction

In Part 1, we reviewed the components of spiritual and moral development in the primary school. The purpose of Part 2 is to explore the central themes that emerged in Part 1 in greater depth and to offer some thoughts on how the principles identified might be applied in practice. We have deliberately written each theme so that it is 'context neutral', in other words it can be applied irrespective of age, ability or cultural inheritance. What we hope is that you will find ideas and stimuli to develop your own approach to meet the needs of your pupils, colleagues and community.

Each theme is developed to provide an overview of the issues and implications that we feel grow out of it. There are three consistent strategies that underpin our approach: dialogue, reflection and facilitation. We believe that these three approaches are essential to effective learning in the context of moral and spiritual learning and growth. These are not just strategies for teachers and adults – a consistent message across the themes is that children and young people need to be active participants in their own development. Children and young people need access to these strategies if the focus of each theme is to be fully understood and translated into personal understanding and practice. Thus 'how' is as important as 'what' and the process of learning becomes an act of empowerment in its own right.

The broad principles of each of these strategies may be summarized as follows:

Dialogue

- A reciprocal and interdependent process growing out of respect, trust and love.
- The shared creation of knowledge rather than the transmission of information – dialogue is a horizontal rather than vertical process.
- A concern for mutual well-being, explicit focus on emotional states and the quality of interaction.
- Contributions are appreciated and valued and built on – 'Yes, and ...' rather than 'Yes, but ...'
- A problem-solving enquiry-based approach which focuses on creative solutions that are based in active consent.

- The participants in the dialogue reflect on the process and work to improve their skills and behaviours.
- There is mutual support, reinforcement, recognition and praise.

Reflection

- Reflection is given status as a fundamental component of any learning process.
- Time and space are built into all learning activities, social processes and projects.
- Reflection is supported by analysis and creative questioning.
- Reflection can be individual or shared, or, ideally, a combination.
- All perspectives are valued and all contributions incorporated.
- Questions and diagnostic pro formas may support the process.
- The outcomes of reflection are used as the basis for future interaction.

Facilitation

- A non-directive approach to enabling group learning.
- The effective facilitator is neutral, it promotes and seeks engagement, and is inclusive.
- Facilitation works through questioning, active listening, synthesizing and summarizing.
- The facilitator models the appropriate behaviours for the group and moves it towards self-management.
- Facilitation moves the group forward by balancing directive and non-directive interventions and balancing affirmation and challenge as appropriate.
- Effective learning in groups requires explicit agreement about shared purpose, common values and agreed protocol.

We would argue that these three strategies have intrinsic value in supporting deep and profound learning but they also have the potential to develop cognitive capacity and act as a personal portfolio of strategies to support spiritual and moral development.

1 A Sense of self

One of the most important factors in spiritual development is the creation in each person of an understanding of their uniqueness, dignity and value as a person. This is the basis for every subsequent topic and is fundamental to any notion of an educated person. There is, of course, a very fine balance between supporting the growth of a valid sense of self and responding to the modern pressures of egocentricity and individualism. Equally there is a delicate relationship between personal autonomy and integrity, and the demands and expectations of others. There is a continual struggle between respecting difference, valuing uniqueness and the expectations of others.

A positive sense of self is essential to a person's physical, psychological, moral and spiritual being. It relates directly to being at ease with oneself, a sense of well-being, and is intrinsic to any notion of happiness. Accepting increasing responsibility for our own well-being is a sign of growing maturity. Living in a state of self-denial and dependency both diminishes and marginalizes us. There are multiple stereotypes which can inhibit human potential, the pressure to conform, or the imposition of expectations can compromise the emergence of an authentic person.

There are many factors that can work to limit and inhibit a child's sense of his or her own value as a person:

- Perceiving themselves to be different by virtue of race, disability, appearance, ability or social acceptance.
- Being an 'outsider', not having a peer group or being deliberately ostracized or marginalized.
- Experiencing sustained negativity, a lack of love and care, and a sense of not being wanted.
- Being the victim of unreasonable expectations and thereby constantly 'failing'.

Any of these factors on their own will have a serious negative impact on the development of a positive and authentic self-image. This in turn will limit growth of moral and spiritual self-awareness.

Moral and spiritual development is rooted in the growing ability to answer the question 'Who am I?' and so develop a sense of responsibility for personal actions and impact on others. Those who have no sense of self will be almost certainly unable to have a sense of others. Failure to support this process or deliberately distort it can possibly result in personal and/or social disfunctionality.

The essential components of a positive sense of self might include:

- A sense of being special, unique and a person in one's own right.
- Recognition and celebration of gifts, talents and contributions.
- Opportunities for success and achievement.
- Being recognized as an individual, for example through the use of one's name.
- Being held personally accountable.
- Having the capacity to make valid choices.
- Being trusted.
- Being loved.

It has to be recognized that there will be multiple alternative expressions of the factors. Each component can be compromised if difference is not celebrated, cherished and seen as a right.

Every teacher knows that using a child's name is the quickest way to secure his or her attention and engagement. Every teacher strives to know the full details of every child they teach, so that they can respond on a personal basis. The movement from generic teaching to supporting the learning of the individual is the quickest way to achieve and secure understanding. So it is with the development of a sense of self.

Schools can be impersonal; the individual can get lost. It is worth reflecting on the experience of a child who goes through a day at school without personal affirmation and then goes home to a similar experience.

There is a range of strategies that can help to enhance a child's sense of self without resorting to artificial, and spurious, devices:

- The habitual use of a child's name – the basis of our sense of identity.
- Focusing on the uniqueness of the school as a community and the uniqueness of every member of the community.
- The celebration of difference. Having a week when everyone is asked to move outside their normal friendship group and explore what they learn from the new friendships
- Opportunities for personally significant success and achievement, for example an annual award for kindness and generosity.
- Public recognition and celebration.
- Opportunities for choice as an expression of individuality.
- Celebrations of birthdays and significant family events.
- 'Touch them every day' – a smile, a wink, greeting by name, a follow-up question to the previous encounter – all stressing recognition and being valued.

2 Understanding right and wrong

What constitutes right and wrong is the pivotal question for the great philosophies, the world's faiths and most aspects of social, political and cultural life. In many ways, learning for understanding through spiritual and moral development (and the core purpose of education) is to help individuals recognize what is right and what is wrong. As was discussed in Chapter 3, there are multiple variations on what constitute the eternal verities – those principles which are absolute, incontrovertible and transcend time and place. In the eighteenth century a child could be hanged for stealing a handkerchief – today even arson in the Royal Dockyards is not a capital offence. Many of the wars of the twentieth century were fought in the name of democracy – with each side believing it was defending democratic principles and that it had 'God on its side'.

Exploring what constitutes right or wrong, moral and immoral behaviour is potentially highly problematic in an age of moral relativism that denies absolutes and sees right behaviour in terms of individual judgement. At the same time we have argued in Chapter 3 that an appeal to power or control is an inappropriate basis for moral development. 'Do as I say' will only produce compliance on the basis of fear of punishment. Equally, it is perfectly proper to explore what is right or wrong in terms of what is legal or illegal – although there is always the danger that what is deemed legal may not be perceived as moral.

The starting point for any discussion on right and wrong is probably best initiated in terms of reason – activities that are based in discussion, explanation, justification and exemplification. The process of reasoning is accompanied by a focus on understanding the implications of beliefs and actions, for example 'If I believe in A then this means …', 'If I do X then this means …'.

Using this approach it becomes possible to explore why certain social prohibitions are in place, for example laws against stealing or violence and to develop a personal engagement and understanding so that acceptance of them is based on consent rather than compliance. Fundamental to this approach is the art of questioning, and central to this is the teacher modelling appropriate questions at every opportunity – and then seeking, reinforcing and celebrating appropriate responses through further questioning:

'Why is it wrong to steal?' 'Why?'

'What would happen if we all stole from each other?' 'Why?'

'Is there a difference between stealing because of need and stealing because of greed?' 'Why?'

"What should happen to people who steal?" "Why?"

'What should be done for the victims of theft?' 'Why?'

'When would it be right to steal?' 'Why?'

'How would you stop people stealing?' 'Why?'

It is the 'Why?' questions that helps to develop understanding. Developing the capacity to explain, rationalize and illustrate is central to achieving personal commitment and consent. Using questions in this way can be traced back to Socrates. Effective and appropriate questioning techniques are among the most powerful strategies for developing an understanding. They need to be modelled by the teacher and consciously and explicitly developed as a classroom strategy. The criteria for such an approach would include using the following range of questions:

Open:

'Why do you think that is true?'

Testing:

'Do you believe that applies in all cases?'

Naive:

'So violence is never justified?'

Clarifying:

'Can you tell me why the First World War was not a just war but the Second World War was?'

Comparing:

'What are the similarities (or differences) between A and B?'

Elaborating:

'Could you give me more examples of that?'

'What does that mean in practice?'

Hypothesizing:

'What would happen if we eliminated poverty?'

'Would it end violent crime?'

Speculative:

'What would happen if everyone did that?'

Focusing:

'Can you give me a concrete example of that?'

Encouraging:

'That's really helpful ... can you give me more examples please?'

Challenging:

'Why do you think that?'

The use of questions is largely determined by context. It also depends on careful listening in order to use the appropriate question and using feedback to confirm understanding. An effective strategy is to agree a number of questions that will be used by all adults in the school when dealing with any behavioural issue. The questions are launched at an assembly and children are actively encouraged to use them in their own interactions. Whatever formulation of questions is used, the final question should focus on the emotional impact of the behaviour and the strategies needed to start healing and recovery. Throughout the process there is an emphasis on whether all those involved feel that they have been listened to and an exploration of the choices involved.

3 Making moral choices

Choice is the means by which we turn spiritual and ethical principles into personal values and hence moral behaviour. The extent to which we can make choices, and our ability to live with the implications of those choices, is the most powerful expression of moral confidence. How we choose determines who we are and how we live – it is the most tangible expression of free will. It is also a direct manifestation of the extent to which we live in a democratic society. Personal happiness is significantly influenced by the choices we make and, in many ways, being educated is about learning what choices are available and how we choose. In many ways it is the ability to choose that makes us human. People are punished by the removal of choice; the law recognizes increasing maturity by making more choices available as we get older.

Leading a moral life and giving full expression to one's spirituality is about making choices. One of the key messages from Chapter 4 is the notion of moving from dependency to interdependency and the extent to which this is reflected in the ability to make real and significant choices. A significant issue in this context is the extent to which individuals are able to make valid choices in their own right. Teachers and parents often use choice as a sanction or reward, rather than as a necessary life skill. The denial or withdrawal of the right to exercise choice has profound implications in terms of self-belief, self-confidence and the development of the capacity to engage in any choice process and the denial of self: 'I can't be trusted to make a decision so I am not worthy of the outcomes of any opportunity to make a decision.'

How rational choices are made is well understood – there is a clear sequence which, in theory, identifies the optimum solution:

Making a good decision
1. What is it that I want to achieve? What are my goals? What problem do I want to solve.

2. What are my priorities? What are the moral implications of my choice?

3. What options are available to me?

4. How close are the options to my goals? Which options meet my moral and spiritual criteria?

5. What is the optimum choice? Which is most likely to achieve my goals, solve the problem?

6. What are the implications of my choice for me, for others, for my options in the future?

7. What have I learned from this process? How did I make my decision? Did it work?

However, no decision is made in isolation, there is never absolute objectivity; the range of options is usually limited and there are many complex variables. The following sequence provides a model which can be adapted to age and context.

Factors influencing choice

THINKING

- Literacy – the ability to articulate the options.
- Problem solving – analytical and prioritizing skills.
- Creativity – innovative thinking.
- Metacognition – learning from the process.

RESOURCES

- Time – the pressure to go through the process.
- Money – the availability of money to make things happen.
- Opportunity – the breadth of options that are available.
- Support – the availability of other people.

PERSONALITY

- Confidence – the combination of knowledge and experience.
- Anxiety and stress – the emotional impact of the process.
- Motivation – how significant is the choice?
- Perseverance – is it worth the commitment?
- Comfort with complexity – the ability to manage ambiguity and the unknown.

EXPERIENCE

- Age – relative maturity and experience.
- Diversity of experiences – being able to draw on previous experience.
- Personal success – what has worked in the past.
- Other people – how will this impact on others?

Making moral choices is essentially about 'doing the right thing' and covers the spectrum from fast food or salad at lunchtime to theft, lying and using violence against another person. Every time we make a moral decision a moral equation comes into play which includes factors such as:

- perceived benefits
- the likelihood of reward or praise
- the possibility of being found out
- the perceived significance of the sanctions
- the implications for future relationships.

How this equation is reconciled is what determines our success or failure in making moral choices.

4 Relationships and respect

It is through our relationships that we express our moral and spiritual self most profoundly. Our relationships are the most direct manifestation of the extent to which we translate principles into practice, in other words the extent to which we are authentic people. Respect can be seen as the expression of authenticity: the recognition of the equal value and worth of others. Our success as social beings is a direct product of the extent to which we are able to create and sustain successful relationships built on respect. This in turn depends on self-acceptance as a prerequisite for self-respect – respecting others begins with self-respect, which in turn grows out of personal security in well-developed relationships.

This raises the issue of emotional literacy, the acknowledgement that our social interactions are based on our emotions and therefore we need to be able to understand how our emotional state determines behaviour and interactions. Being in school involves a wide range of opportunities for success or failure in terms of social interaction, and a great deal of the work of teachers centres on managing the complex range of emotions that comes into the classroom each day. Any understanding of effective relationships that are based in respect might therefore be based on a range of criteria or a set of protocols for living and working together. According to Goleman (2006) the components of social intelligence are:

Social Awareness

Social awareness refers to a spectrum that runs from instantaneously sensing another's inner state, to understanding her feelings and thoughts, to 'getting' complicated social situations. It includes:

- *Primal empathy*: Feeling with others; sensing non-verbal emotional signals.

- *Attunement*: Listening with full receptivity; attuning to a person.

- *Empathic accuracy*: Understanding another person's thoughts, feelings, and intentions.

- *Social cognition*: Knowing how the social world works.

Social Facility

Simply sensing how another feels, or knowing what they think or intend, does not guarantee fruitful interactions. Social facility builds on social awareness to allow smooth, effective interactions. The spectrum of social facility includes:

- *Synchrony*: Interacting smoothly at the nonverbal level.

- *Self-presentation*: Presenting ourselves effectively.

- *Influence*: Shaping the outcome of social interactions.

- *Concern*: Caring about others' needs and acting accordingly. (page 84)

The practical manifestations of social intelligence include:

- active listening
- sensitive to body language
- giving feedback
- articulating emotional states
- allowing silence
- open and supportive questions
- appropriate physical contact
- reinforcing through 'mirroring' behaviour.

Teachers can help to develop and sustain effective relationships by:

- Modelling appropriate behaviours – this is perhaps the most powerful strategy – children develop much of their social behaviour by copying adults. In particular, staff can model active listening through assembly and then by making explicit reference whenever appropriate.

- Building a shared vocabulary in the classroom to reinforce appropriate attitudes and behaviours, and to support dialogue around relationships.

- Facilitating regular conversations exploring the emotional impact and implications of positive and negative behaviours with staff not being afraid to display emotions in front of children.

- Recognizing and publicly celebrating appropriate behaviours. Each week a child can be identified who has modelled appropriate behaviour, his or her photograph is displayed, with a letter home and a mention in the school newsletter.

- Using story, drama and scenarios to explore the emotional impact of the positive and negative aspects of relationships.

- Drawing explicit links between individual behaviour and school values and protocols.

- Ensuring that relationships and mutual respect are regular themes of review and reflection by the class (see Theme 13).

Central to any work on relationships and respect is the experience of friendship and it is through the experience of friendship that most children learn to explore relationships outside their immediate family ties. Childhood friendships ebb and flow, best friends will become implacable enemies and friends again within hours. Friendship can be a brutal weapon of exclusion. The constant evolution of friendship groups determines much of the social reality of the classroom. Friendship therefore provides a powerful vehicle for exploring the basis of relationships and respect. An obvious challenge in any social situation, although especially in schools, is engaging with the 'hard-to-like'. Moving from the charitable or indulgent represents a substantial leap in attitudes, values and practice.

5 Empathy and compassion

Compassion is perhaps the greatest of all virtues; it is what makes us truly human. In many ways, compassion underlies most of the definitions and understanding of the nature of humanity. To behave in an inhuman way is to act without regard for the rights, feelings and sensibilities of others. Compassion is the most powerful expression of our moral sense with regard to other people. In its focus on the needs and wants of others it is also an expression of a spiritual understanding that moves beyond self, however this can be so easily blocked by personal insecurities and inflated egos. To be compassionate is to demonstrate a heightened and sophisticated awareness of the integrity of another person.

Such a disposition is rooted in empathy – the ability to engage with another human being on their terms. The essential characteristics of empathy can be defined as:

- The ability to understand and internally replicate the situation of another person.
- The ability to recognize and understand one's own emotional states and then respond appropriately to similar states in others.
- The ability to translate awareness and understanding into appropriate responses and actions.
- An understanding of the relationship between understanding another person and what constitutes 'correct' responses.

The development of empathy in children and young people allows for the expression of compassion and, in perhaps its highest expression, altruism. Altruistic behaviour is the most significant expression of empathy and compassion – we usually understand it through some form of personal sacrifice which denies self in favour of others. In many ways, the moral and spiritual acts we most value and revere are those involving the 'ultimate sacrifice'. This has to be viewed with caution, as motivation is all important in this context. Is an act genuinely self-less or self-gratifying?

According to Goleman (1996) children are empathic from infancy:

> The moment Hope, just nine months old, saw another baby fall, tears welled up in her own eyes and she crawled off to be comforted by her mother, as though it were she who had been hurt. And fifteen-month-old Michael went to get his own teddy bear for his crying friend Paul: when Paul kept crying, Michael retrieved Paul's security blanket for him. Both these small acts of sympathy and caring were observed by mothers trained to record such incidents of empathy in action. (page 98)

The development of this capacity is one of the foundations of moral and spiritual development. Mason and Dearden (2004) provide an example of how mutual empathy develops into a sophisticated social relationship:

> 'I have a friend who is disabled. He is called Dominic. We were in nursery together. He joined our school this year and we got really close. Sometimes I feed him at lunchtime. You know when you meet that person they'll always be a friend … I understand him, the way he feels, he understands me and the way I feel. He does things to cheer me up … he'll do something funny, make a face to make me laugh.' Kirsty, Kirkhill Primary School (page 14)

There is, of course, a danger that empathy and compassion might be expressed as pity. A group of disabled young people were playing on a beach. The response of many passers-by or families also on the beach was to offer money to the teacher and then move their families away. Was this motivated by empathy and compassion or by pity? Pity is motivated by sadness; it is essentially a negative response which places the pitied person in a negative context rather than affirming a shared humanity. Rather than offering money, the passers-by might have encouraged their own children to play with the disabled children Their behaviour also fuels the stereotype that disabled people are somehow jealous/envious of their non-disabled peers because of what they 'lack' and cannot experience happiness because of their difference. Pity can be motivated by a sense of superiority. (Example provided by Ingrid Bradbury.)

The problem with pity is that is has become the most widely used, and exploited, response to the suffering of others. Television advertisements for a range of entirely worthy causes exploit pity as an emotional response and we react, and salve our consciences, by sending money. Schools respond to man-made and natural disasters by fund-raising and there is no doubt that this is valid and worthy. However, it may be educating children into a response based on pity (sadness) rather than compassion (empathy). The issue is one of authenticity – compassion is based on shared humanity, pity on 'there but for the grace of God …' If the response to a tsunami or earthquake is to give money, then there is a danger that we might be educating children into symbolic responses. A case in point is the bully who gives money to the charity appeal but sees no relationship to his behaviour in the playground. Giving money to charity can lead to self-congratulation and a denial of the need to take more fundamental action, for example paying higher taxes to help eliminate child poverty.

The development of compassion through empathy is central to any model of moral and spiritual development. Empathy and compassion are challenging concepts because they require us to abandon the natural instincts of self-interest and self-preservation. There is a fundamental debate about the extent to which children can be empathic and compassionate because they appear at odds with what we know of the natural and normal focus on self. Empathy and compassion are higher-order feelings – essentially the ability to move beyond seeing the world exclusively on our terms and engage with human beings on their terms. Empathy and compassion involve participation in the pain, grief and distress of others.

In terms of personal spiritual and moral growth and learning it is important to explore these virtues in terms of personal immediacy and response. Perhaps the most challenging aspect of this is to explore the differences between pity and compassion, and this is perhaps best done through exploring scenarios. For example:

What are the differences between empathy, compassion and pity for a disabled person?

How does the person feeling pity feel? What do they do?

What would be the difference in being compassionate?

Is it possible to empathize with a disabled person?

The obvious learning strategy here is to ask a disabled child or adult to articulate his or her responses to the ways in which people respond to them. The following extract from Mason and Dearden (2004) provides an example of how a child at an infant school can articulate his or her responses to being with a disabled child:

'What we most enjoy at playtime is when we push William up the hill in his wheelchair and come down really fast – we run down all holding on because we must not let go or he will roll off and get hurt. We hold on really tight in case he gets frightened. We enjoy reading with William. We hold out two books and he looks at the one he wants. We follow his eyes. He likes Kipper books. Lucy and Vita hold the book and turn the pages. Natasha reads the words. When he is out of his wheelchair he lies down to take part in activities and we lie down with him. When William goes to soft play a group of us go with him and we all roll around together. The best thing about having William in the class is his hugging and giving big cuddles.' Child, Davigdor Infants School (page 12)

Empathy and compassion involve participation in joy, happiness, pain, grief and distress of others,' – children and staff are not afraid to show and share those feelings as in the following example:

A teacher shared some music with us in assembly that had been her and new husband's song when they first met. She described how the new relationship had 'healed' her. Another staff member shared music that she had listened to when nursing her newly born baby. Another staff member shared the music her mother had wanted playing at her funeral. This led to how we cope when people/things we love are not there any more. The children shared their experiences quite openly.

In this example, the teachers were being open about their feelings and relationships – the use of music is a powerful reinforcing factor. The teachers were being authentic and genuine and thus inviting empathic responses. It is difficult to envisage how this might be achieved other than through real-life examples – children would rapidly spot the artificial or contrived. Openness inspires confidence and 'gives permission' to replicate that behaviour.

It could be argued that a lack of empathy is the basis for most negative behaviour towards another human being. Physical and verbal aggression, theft and actions that cause hurt or offence are only possible because of a lack of awareness of the impact of that behaviour. The often repeated question 'How would you feel if someone did that to you?' is usually pointless because it is the inability to think this way that led to the behaviour.

Bullying is a classic example of behaviour that has its roots in a inability to empathize – bullies behave in the way they do because they have no sense of the impact of their actions on others.

A strategy to address this type of behaviour that is increasingly being used in schools is the concept of restorative justice. Based originally on a Maori social strategy, it works on the basis of developing understanding and recognition of behaviour rather than simply punishing. The principles of restorative justice can be summarized as follows:

1. Enabling the offending individual an opportunity to understand the impact of his or her behaviour on others.
2. Providing the victim with a secure environment to confront the offending individual and explain the impact and implications of his or her actions.
3. Developing strategies to prevent the behaviour happening again and to establish protocols.
4. Establishing clear responsibilities and accountabilities.

Fundamental to restorative justice is ensuring that the victim feels safe by challenging the inappropriate behaviour (rather than punishing the offender), getting the offender to accept personal responsibility and so minimize the possibility of similar behaviour in the future. The whole process hinges on the articulation of feelings and the development of strategies to build mutual confidence in the future. It is a classic example of prevention being better than cure:

Belinda Hopkins, of the National Centre for Restorative Justice in Education, sees the approach as a whole new way of doing things, 'The traditional, authoritarian, punitive environment of the school is dangerous to young people,' she says. 'If you threaten youngsters with the consequences of wrongdoing, what you mean is the consequences to themselves – you are teaching them not to get caught. We want kids to do the right things for the right reasons. We want to teach them empathy.' (Gibbs, 2007, pages 6–7)

The impact on all participants can be profound:

Several boys expressed acute remorse at the part they had taking in the bullying – one even expressed guilt at having stood by passively. The conference ended with an exploration of how matters could be put right.

This shift of emphasis away from punitive action makes the school safer, especially for vulnerable pupils. Jerry was relieved Karl wasn't suspended for bullying him. 'I don't think him not coming to school would have been an answer – it was better to work it out there and then than go though the whole thing of you being scared when he comes back,' he says. (Gibbs, 2007, page 7)

Restorative justice is a powerful example of a practical strategy to build empathy and compassion into the daily life of the school. Crucially it is being learned rather than taught.

Fairness, 6 equity and inclusion

Fairness is one of the most significant criteria that children apply to their experience of school. Their innate sense of justice recognizes that equity and inclusion are basic principles that determine the integrity of any organization. However, we often do not engage with the difference between unequal and unfair. Fairness, equity and inclusion in schools cover a variety of issues that range from the banal to the profound. Access to a favourite toy in the reception class is an issue of fairness to those unable to get near the sand table. Failure to demonstrate parity of esteem to all children in Year 6, irrespective of perceived ability or educability, is an issue of fundamental human rights. There will be many causes of such a situation, from the personal attitudes and behaviours of the teacher, to the prevailing culture in the community, to the institutionalized discrimination in the design and assessment of the curriculum.

The most basic questions centre on the nature of the educational process – 'What does it mean to educate someone fairly?', 'How do we secure genuine equality of opportunity?' and 'How do we create an inclusive community?'. These are profound questions that shape our understanding of schools, the curriculum, and the roles of teachers and pupils. The issue is one of process and outcomes – how do we design an educational system that is ethical and inclusive both in the way it works as well as in what it produces? Even in the most democratic and egalitarian of schools there are structural, attitudinal and cultural forces that deny the possibility of equity and inclusion.

The prevailing norms and structures around us provide a justification for hierarchy. Our individualistic and organizational need to rank, prioritize and position lead us to perpetuate an education system that produces more of the same discriminatory behaviour and ensuing undemocratic processes. The system needs to get fairer not better; the focus on improvement may actually have worked against equity.

If we identify our personal philosophy as aspiring to equity and inclusion, we need to recognize that this is at odds with the process and outcomes of our learning environments. Our learning communities are failing a number of people by perpetuating processes that fuel inequality and discrimination. The absence of clear leadership on equality makes us as responsible for injustice as perpetrating physical harm to the groups we marginalize.

Selection and streaming, for example, might be justified on short-term, expedient, grounds but have significant ethical implications in the broader scheme of things. Opposition to inclusion begs many significant ethical questions. Inevitably, in a complex society, responses will be couched with caveats and a hierarchy of significance and the 'greatest happiness' argument may well be adopted. The danger is one of ethical relativism, adopting a stance because it is the least objectionable or because it comes closest to achieving compromise. What is clear is that the school system continues to perpetuate many of the fundamental discriminatory trends in society on the basis of gender, ethnicity, disability, poverty and social class. Our language around *minorities and needs* perpetuates deficiency thinking as status quo and, in so doing, makes acceptable the very existence of whole communities as an underclass. We expect a percentage of failure within the system, so that those achieving only do so by contrast. The present system models impeccably the core belief that the people within it are in fact of unequal value. The dominant model of accountability influencing schools is one of academic performance. The challenge of Every Child Matters is to find performance criteria that see academic success as only one measure of personal and organizational effectiveness.

These are ethical perspectives which have to be clarified, codified into a personal value system and then applied in the day-to-day life of a school. Schools are moral communities, there is no aspect of school life that does not have an ethical antecedent, all decisions are based on personal value systems and the morality of the school is expressed through the daily concrete experiences of all its members. It is impossible to separate the educational process from ethical considerations as the decision to educate is, of itself, an ethical decision.

Mason and Dearden (2004) argue that:

> It is not easy to describe a fully inclusive school because there are none yet. However, there are many early years centres, schools and colleges that are trying to do things differently in all sorts of new and exciting ways. These places of learning have certain things in common:
>
> **They** believe that all children need to feel that they are wanted and belong to their local community.
>
> **They** believe that all children can think and can learn.
>
> **They** believe in building on what children can do, not on their weaknesses or impairments.

They believe that children need help, not punishment, when their behaviour gets out of control.

They believe that difference is something to welcome and to learn from.

They respect young people.

They empower young people.

They involve parents.

They do not think treating people equally means treating them the same.

They see schools as a resource to families and to the local community.

They apply their thinking about inclusion to the staff as well as the children.
(pages 8–9)

It may be worth involving pupils, adults and parents in an audit of the extent to which they perceive the school to be inclusive, inviting their responses to questions such as:

- Is this an open and welcoming school for everyone?
- Is physical access easy for everyone?
- Are resources managed equitably?
- Is there active and equal participation in all aspects of school life?
- What is the status of the inclusion policy?
- Is there professional development to support the policy?
- Is there real partnership with the community?
- Is there active collaboration with all interested parties?
- Are all of the above monitored?
- Is there a willingness to intervene to secure equity?

(This theme draws on ideas developed by Laura Chapman.)

7 Democracy and participation

Democracy is one of the most powerful expressions of the ethical basis of most modern societies. The right to participate in government, however indirectly, is a hard-won right which encapsulates the modern history of many countries. Being a citizen in a modern democracy is the basis for many of the defining characteristics of modern life:

- The ability to vote in elections at local and national level.
- The right to hold and express a range of beliefs and opinions.
- The right to assemble, form and join a range of organizations.
- The right to enjoy freedom from discrimination based on gender, ethnicity, faith, age and disability.

Such rights are, of course, accompanied by a range of responsibilities – notably the obligation to obey the law, pay taxes and participate fully in the civic life of community and society. Schools can never be democratic in the same way in which hospitals, businesses, the armed forces and so on can never be fully democratic according to our prevailing cultural and political norms. However, all organizations can be participative and work to secure the involvement of their members.

There is a real danger that schools will teach democracy and participation as subjects rather than allowing young people to learn about them through real and valid participation. Engagement with democratic principles and creating opportunities for authentic participation are necessary to develop the school as an ethical community and provide a practical focus for moral education.

According to Burke and Grosvenor (2003) there is a real demand for greater involvement in how schools are run:

My need is now, today ... Teach me not to be apathetic, share your wisdom, listen to my ideals. Susan

I don't think I would get on very well in my ideal school because I am too used to being told what to do. Frances

In my ideal school ... we will no longer be treated like herds of an identical animal waiting to be civilised before we are let loose on the world. It will be recognised that it is our world too.

Miriam

As pupils we are able to create

An atmosphere of freedom.

We are willing and eager

To express our thoughts.

Our school is a place where

Children are free to be a child.

Jayne (pages 7–8)

The essence of contemporary political theories about democracy is that the ability to make decisions should be located with those who are most likely to be influenced by the decisions. In other words, there should be movement from consultation to participation whenever it is practical and possible. There are obvious issues to do with relevance, maturity and appropriateness as to what might be handed over to young people, but it is probably fair to say that many schools underestimate the capacity and ability of their pupils to make valid decisions:

> One point that emerges quite strongly in our pupil data is that young people's experiences of life outside school often contrast sharply with their experiences within school. These differences can give young people the impression that school is a 'world apart' and therefore what happens in the classroom is seen, to some extent, as irrelevant. ... Many find their personal interests, experience and capabilities are not recognised or valued in the classroom. (Flutter and Rudduck, 2004, page 132)

> Giving young people more opportunities to say what they think about schooling and developing their sense of responsibility as members of a learning community represents moves towards a different construction of the pupil role. Rather than being seen as dependent and incapable, pupils are regarded as individuals possessing the right to be heard and to be respected as well as the responsibility to act in ways that align with the best interests of their school community. (ibid., page 134)

Flutter and Rudduck (2004) quote Cooper (1996, page 206):

> One thing that has been made clear by researchers over the past thirty years is that school pupils (and often those considered to be disaffected, maladjusted or otherwise deviant) are astute and insightful critics of schools and schooling … We ignore their insights to the detriment of our schools, the future of our pupils and the future of our society. (page 138)

The possible levels of consultation and participation are reflected in Figure 7.1.

---

4. pupils as fully active participants and co-researchers
pupils and teachers jointly initiate enquiry; pupils play an active role in decision making; together with teachers, they plan action in the light of data and review impact of the intervention.

3. pupils as researchers
pupils are involved in enquiry and have an active role in decision making; there will be feedback and discussion with pupils regarding findings drawn from the data.

2. pupils as active participants
teachers initiate enquiry and interpret the data but pupils students are taking some role in decision making; there is likely to be some feedback to on the findings drawn from the data.

1. listening to pupils
pupils are a source of data; teachers respond to data but pupils are not involved in discussion of findings; there may be no feedback to pupils; teachers act on the data.

0. pupils not consulted
there is no element of pupil participation or pupil consultation within the school.

Figure 7.1 The ladder of pupil participation (Flutter and Rudduck, 2004, page 16, with permission from RoutledgeFalmer)

Against each of these five levels it is possible to identify a range of processes and activities that pupils might be involved in to a greater or lesser extent:

1. Year groups being given responsibility for part of the school site and being given a budget to design and implement their plan and to maintain their plot.
2. Membership of the school council is extended to all ages and a wider range of issues being considered – notably the quality of teaching and learning.

3. Involving students in staff appointment procedures.

4. Developing students as counsellors, mentors and tutors to support the learning of other students and to be actively involved in managing behaviour, for example in facilitating restorative justice conferences.

5. Students being given real management roles in the planning and delivery of school projects, for example trips, overseas visits.

Perhaps the greatest challenge would be to introduce full participation into the classroom giving students a substantial and authentic voice in deciding what, where, when and how they learn, and even who they learn with. Such choices, as with all the examples listed above, assume the development of an ability to choose (see Theme 3). They also assure a range of skills and strategies:

1. Analysis and problem solving.

2. Listening and giving feedback.

3. Proposing strategies and building on the proposals of others.

4. Negotiating and influencing to achieve consensus.

5. Generating alternative solutions.

6. Explaining and clarifying.

7. Exploring and understanding options.

8. Securing agreement and commitment.

9. Establishing accountability – who does what, when?

These strategies are as appropriate to the primary and special school council as they are to a meeting of the Cabinet in 10 Downing Street (although they are more likely to be more meaningful in the former). Such behaviours are needed in every walk of life and at all levels. Education for democracy requires that they should be implicit to school life and lived in practice rather than taught in theory. Giving students opportunities to be involved in real projects involving manufacturing goods, providing services on an economic basis, can provide powerful learning opportunities, especially if there are links with local businesses and service providers.

8 The natural world

In many ways our engagement with the natural world is one of the most powerful sources of spiritual insight and inspiration. How we engage with the world is emerging as a dominant moral issue – and one that children and young people have a natural affinity with. The strategy of one infant and nursery school to ensure that every child has the opportunity to hold a newborn lamb opens the door to so many spiritual and moral possibilities:

- The miracle of new life.
- The gentleness and vulnerability of the lambs.
- The fact that they will be slaughtered and eaten.
- The relationship between humans and animals.
- The realities of birth and death.

Holding a lamb may be the start of a process that responds to O'Sullivan's (1999) challenge:

> … We are in need of a spirituality whose scope and magnitude will open us up to the wonder and the joy of the universe. We are in need of a spirituality which has embedded within it a biocentric vision that keeps us vitally connected to the natural world and to the unfolding of the universe. We need an enchanted spirituality that awakens us to the awesome quality of our experience within this grand mystery that we have been born into. We need an embodied spirituality that connects our bodies to the deep mystery of things. (page 264)

The current growing debate around environmental issues is providing a forum for moral, spiritual and political debate. In many ways it represents the most elemental of issues with the very future of the planet as the motivation for action. For Tacey (2003):

... In a sense, ecospirituality is not about words, it is about experiences. It is about moments of passion, peace and belonging, and because these rewards are so profound, they are also priceless and beyond reckoning. But we cannot expect to achieve a constant 'high' in nature, only moments of recognition, where we remember who we are ... It is from these fleeting experiences that we find strength to face the ordinary disappointments, and develop a sense of security that can sustain us through the various trials of life. (page 188)

Throughout history, the natural world has provided some of the most powerful and compelling opportunities for spiritual insight and moral choice. Spiritual meaning might become an almost visceral understanding of interdependence: a deep and profound connection to each other, to animals, to plants and to every dimension of the planet. If we are to be interdependent at these levels, then equity becomes even more important because our happiness and well-being are tied up with the connection to each element and not just recognizing and being aware of another's needs. We should be aware of:

- The power and majesty of a thunderstorm.
- The transformation of a snowfall.
- The glory of a sunset combined with the vibrant colours of autumn.
- The softness of rain and the exuberance of jumping into puddles.
- The hope that goes with the first hint of green in the spring.
- The impact of a landscape of trees, rocks and water.
- The cathedral-like quality of woodland in high summer.
- The destruction of a meadow to build a bypass.
- The systematic abuse of livestock raised in battery conditions to provide cheap food.
- The cynical pollution of rivers in the name of industrial efficiency.
- The paradox of thousands of people visiting a beauty spot in their cars.

It is these contradictions that seem to have mobilized the interest, compassion and anger of many children and young people. Interestingly, there is often an almost pantheistic, Wordsworthian view of the natural world which finds the divine in nature as well as a sense of injustice and anxiety about the long-term viability of the world's ecosystems.

Whatever its causes, global warming is potentially one of the most significant factors in determining the future lives of children in school. It would therefore seem reasonable to give it high status in any educational programme, not just in terms of citizenship or geography, but rather as one of the central moral issues and a challenge that requires a spiritual as well as political response. The evidence for climatic change is overwhelming, yet modern societies seem unable to act – this may be because the issue is primarily seen in terms of global politics rather than personal, moral and spiritual choices. Consider the following fragments of evidence – assembled at random:

- Wild bears in northern Spain have stopped hibernating – there is enough food for them to stay awake all winter.

- The first commercial olive grove has been planted in Cornwall. Commercial quantities of Cornish extra virgin olive oil will be available soon.

- Many ski resorts in the Swiss Alps will have no snow in winter in the near future.

- 20 of the 21 hottest years on record have occurred in the past 25 years.

- Ospreys and swallows, which normally migrate to Africa, were seen in Suffolk in December 2006.

- Red Admiral butterflies, which normally hibernate in winter, have been breeding in January.

- Polar bears could be extinct in the wild by 2030.

- The perennial Arctic ice – the area that does not melt in summer – reduced by 14 per cent in 2005/2006.

Martin (2006) argues:

> Today's young people will be the generation that brings about this great transition. Let's refer to it as the 21C Transition. They are ultimately responsible for the changes we describe – a transition unlike any before in history. They are the Transition Generation. It is vital that they – all of them – understand the 21C Transition, so that they can understand the critical role they will play. For many, understanding the nature of the 21st century will give meaning to their own lives. (page 5)

It is Martin's last point 'give meaning' that points to ways forward for schools. The issue is to combine the small practical steps that most schools are taking with a focus on environmental issues from a moral and spiritual perspective. It is important to move from recycling as good practice to recycling as a moral act which contributes to spiritual understanding. Possible strategies for schools might include:

- Pupils leading on conservation strategies:
    - Recycling
    - Energy conservation
    - The school environment
    - Wildlife areas.
- Walking to school schemes.
- Partnering with a school in the developing world.
- Forest school schemes.
- Supporting community initiatives.

- Using philosophy for schools to explore moral issues and relate these to practical projects.
- Developing whole school projects on specific environmental themes or areas in crisis, for example Alaska or Vanuatu.

A powerful and practical example of strategies to engage children and young people is the Roots and Shoots movement launched by the noted zoologist Jane Goodall. The mission and goals of the movement demonstrate the relationship between spiritual and moral understanding and taking action.

Our mission: to foster respect and compassion for all living things, to promote understanding of all cultures and beliefs and to inspire each individual to take action to make the world a better place for people, animals and the environment.

Our goals are global:

- To implement positive change through active learning about, caring for and interacting with the environment.
- To demonstrate care and concern for all animals.
- To enhance understanding among individuals of different cultures, ethnic groups, religions, socio-economic levels and nations through our global communications network.
- To help young people develop self-respect, confidence in themselves and hope for the future.

Roots and Shoots provides children with a framework for organizing and achieving meaningful projects that connect their minds, hearts and hands as they promote care and concern for animals, people and the planet. Youth are empowered by the Roots and Shoots model – knowledge, compassion, action – which teaches them they are capable of improving the status quo. Given the overwhelming global crises we face, this contextual framework and genuine youth empowerment is crucial for youth to develop a constructive, participatory and hopeful world view.

9 Happiness

This theme serves as a bridge between the first eight themes, which focused on public and moral issues, and the remaining five, which focus on the personal and the spiritual. Happiness is often, in an idealized and romantic view, seen as axiomatic to childhood – 'the happiest days of our lives' is the well-worn cliché. In many ways, happiness might be seen as the pivotal theme of this book. In advocating 'education for understanding' we are arguing for the optimizing of happiness through a model of education that focuses on the whole person – as a social/moral entity and as a spiritual being with an inner life that feeds, and is fed by, the public self. What is clear is that there are many variant views on access to happiness: marginalized groups in society are expected to accept a modified or diluted form of happiness. Like beauty, happiness has to be defined by the beholder.

As was argued in Chapter 1, happiness is more than the absence of pain or unhappiness. Nor is it about material possessions – people in the West are wealthier and more economically secure than at any time in history yet we are no happier. There are many variables that will inform our happiness:

> There is also an inner, personal factor. Happiness depends not only on our external situation and relationships; it depends on our attitudes as well. From his experiences in Auschwitz, Viktor Frankl concluded that in the last resort 'everything can be taken from a man but one thing, the last of human freedoms – to choose one's attitude in any given set of circumstances.' (Layard, 2005, page 8)

Thus, liberty may be lost but freedom is always available: happiness is a personal disposition. Perhaps one of the most depressing publications in recent times was the UNICEF report, *An Overview of Child Well-being in Rich Countries* (2007). One of the categories analysed was 'subjective well-being': in essence happiness. Although the analysis of the data is contentious it shows:

… that children's subjective sense of well-being appears to be markedly higher in the Netherlands, Spain and Greece and markedly lower in Poland and the United Kingdom. (UNICEF, 2007, page 35)

In fact, children in the UK come twentieth out of 20 in the league table of subjective well-being. Overall, child well-being is highest in the Netherlands with Scandinavian and Mediterranean countries appearing in the top third; the USA and the UK occupy the bottom two places, which seems a sad indictment of the first and fifth wealthiest nations on Earth. This confirmation of Layard's view, quoted above, points to a need for the focus to be on aspects of happiness that are inner and personal.

The rest of this section will explore the contributions schools can make to children's happiness using the criteria developed by Martin (2005), outlined in Chapter 1. One immediate problem is that, according to the UNICEF report (page 36) only 19 per cent of children in the UK 'like school a lot'. Presumably their happiness would be immediately improved by a strategy that is outside the remit of this discussion. Some of the criteria for happiness as identified by Martin are identified elsewhere in this section – what follows is a discussion of the distinctive elements not discussed in the other themes.

Connectedness

A dominant factor in the happiness of children is the quality and integrity of personal relationships – notably with their parents, siblings, members of their extended families and significant friends. It seems to be the depth and quality of these relationships that appears to make the difference. Meaningful relationships build confidence and security. While schools can do very little about the quality of family life, there are perhaps opportunities to enable and cultivate friendships by deliberately focusing on friendship as a key experience of school.

Freedom from excessive anxiety

Anxiety is corrosive and can do much to compromise the possibility of happiness. Schools have significant potential to both create and alleviate anxiety. Possible sources of anxiety generated by life in school might include:

- New and unfamiliar situations, for example not understanding instructions.
- Conflict and tension, for example misunderstandings with a teacher or other pupils.

- Change, for example the move from Foundation to Key Stage 1 to Key Stage 2 or the transfer to secondary school.
- Failure, for example the pressures that are generated by end of Key Stage 2 tests.

Effective teachers will recognize the manifestations of anxiety and intervene appropriately. The use of reflection (Theme 12) and consultation (Theme 7) will often help to identify and alleviate unjustified anxiety.

The quality of working life has a direct impact on happiness. For children this means engaging in learning for understanding as explored in Chapter 4. Children's happiness in school will be increased if the work they do is:

- Appropriate to their personal stage of development.
- Based in problem solving and challenge.
- Focused on social interaction.
- Expressed in a range of meaningful activities.
- Focused on personal achievement.

(Such a culture would also, we suspect, increase teachers' happiness as well.)

A sense of control

People in general, and children as they mature, are more likely to be happy if they do not perceive themselves to be victims of the capriciousness of others. Empowered people who have a sense of control over their lives tend to be happier than those who are at the mercy of others. Education is often guilty of labelling some groups as intrinsically 'unable' and tends to infantilize them.

For children in school this means:

- Opportunities to make valid and significant choices about their lives in school.
- A sense of personal autonomy and dignity.
- Personal space and time.
- A sense of control over key aspects of daily life.

Humour

Humour and fun are pivotal to happiness. Laughter is psychologically and physiologically good for us – humour is a crucial expression and cause of happiness. Humour also has the potential to create trust and connection, and so enable sharing.

Children's positive memories of teachers are often directly linked to smiles, laughter and a sense of fun: always assuming that the boundaries are clear and understood. This is neither to argue for a national standard for humour in the classroom, nor to require every teacher to tell a daily joke, but to recognize a shared humour:

> … can certainly reduce the biological effects of stress, as measured by changes in the levels of the stress-related hormones adrenaline and cortisol. Research has also confirmed that humour in the workplace is correlated with better working relationships, greater job satisfaction and increased productivity. The most creative and productive parts of an organisation are often the noisiest.

Humour is a social lubricant which can help to forge relationships and strengthen existing ones. As such, it promotes connectedness, the most important of all building blocks of happiness. (Martin, 2005, page 65)

Playfulness

We ignore the importance of play at our peril. Watching any wildlife programme will show how vital play is to the social development of animals – from polar bear cubs to meerkats and lambs. Play is part of education. The readiness to engage in play is a powerful indicator of happiness, play also seems to reinforce and extend happiness. Play is essential to the happiness of five- and 50-year-olds. Sport is play, socializing is play, being together is play, mimicking adult behaviour is play.

Schools have made huge strides in moving from supervised standing around at break times to focused and structured play, which has the following characteristics:

The seven play objectives

Objective 1
The provision extends the choice and control that children have over their play, the freedom they enjoy and the satisfaction they gain from it.

Objective 2
The provision recognises the child's need to test boundaries and responds positively to that need.

Objective 3
The provision manages the balance between the need to offer risk and the need to keep children safe from harm.

Objective 4
The provision maximises the range of play opportunities.

Objective 5
The provision fosters independence and self-esteem.

Objective 6

The provision fosters children's respect for others and offers opportunities for social interaction.

Objective 7

The provision fosters the child's well-being, healthy growth and development, knowledge and understanding, creativity and capacity to learn.

(National Playing Fields Association, 2000)

20 things a child should do by the age of 16.

1.	Roll down a grassy bank	11.	Build a collection of …
2.	Play with puppets	12.	Cook a family meal
3.	Make a tree house	13.	Cuddle a lamb
4.	Hands and feet painting	14.	Grow and eat vegetables
5.	Organize a teddy bears' picnic	15.	Play Pooh sticks
6.	Have a face-painting session	16.	Make and fly a kite
7.	Make snow angels	17.	Plant a tree
8.	Camp out overnight in the garden	18.	Sing in a choir
9.	Plan an expedition	19.	Learn to swim
10.	Learn magic tricks	20.	See the stars at night

It would be wonderful to think of the above list as an entitlement for every primary school pupil – as well as many teenagers and not a few adults.

10 Hope and optimism

Hope and optimism are fundamental to personal growth and development. They provide a *raison d'être* for spiritual and moral development in that they offer a focus on a better future. Hope is often seen as an aspirational emotional state and optimism as a more reserved and calculated state but they both emphasize how things might be and so move us beyond our present state. In Greek mythology, when Pandora opened her box she released all the forces influencing the world except one – hope. (The Greeks were suspicious of hope, regarding it as dangerous.) Without hope humanity was filled with despair. It was only when Pandora opened her box again and released hope that humanity was able to cope. Hope was seen as the most potent of the forces influencing human life.

In the teachings of the Roman Catholic Church, hope is seen as one of the three great virtues (with faith and charity). Hope is best thought of as a state of mind that engages with a preferred future which has qualities and attributes which transcend the current situation or has certain characteristics which are ideal, or utopian, or represent an optimum state of being.

Hope is elemental to any concept of childhood – indeed many adults find their most direct experience of hope in their aspirations for their own children or those they work with. Such hope might be expressed in positive aspirations – such as Every Child Matters – or in the avoidance of negatives, for example illness or tragedy. The language of children is often focused on the future – 'how I want to be'. In some ways the role of the educator and parent could be seen as helping to translate utopian hope into well-grounded optimism. Hope in education is often expressed through aspirations and expectations – what is clear is that hope is directly linked with happiness: a life without hope is a life that is literally pointless. For Vaclav Havel hope is:

> … an orientation of the spirit, an orientation of the heart … It is not the conviction that something will turn out well, but the certainty that something makes sense, regardless of how it turns out. (1990, page 181)

Rabbi Jonathan Sacks argues that morality:

> … is the language of hope, for it presupposes that in a critical respect, man is not a part of nature. Because we are speakers of a language we are capable of imagination, of envisaging a reality other than that currently present to the senses. So, for us, there is a difference between 'is' and 'ought', between the world we observe and the world to which we aspire, and in aspiring being to make. (2000, page 266)

Hope has intrinsic merit, the object of hope does not have to be valid, sensible or achievable – engagement with hope is, of itself, appropriate. Hope is the highest state of spiritual and moral expression because it implies a readiness to change and a commitment to growth and so learning. Hope is about the adventure of being alive and the possibility of becoming.

The Invitation

It doesn't interest me what you do for a living.
I want to know what you ache for
and if you dare to dream of meeting your heart's longing.

It doesn't interest me how old you are.
I want to know if you will risk looking like a fool
for love
for your dream
for the adventure of being alive.

(Oriah, www.oriahmountaindreamer.com)

Engagement in what might be called utopian dialogues is essential to any social interaction. It is fundamentally important to articulate a desired future, for it then starts to be attainable, and to benefit from the nurturing and caring that comes from sharing hope. The committed parent, teacher, friend or lover enhances the quality of the relationship and builds a shared future by sharing conversations about hope and then helping to move towards optimism. Utopian dialogues create, clarify, enrich, develop and, ultimately, give life to our dreams and aspirations. It is through caring conversations that we are most likely to understand what it means to hope and how to translate such hope into a life that is lived and is worth living.

Utopian dialogues are found in every dimension of authentic and effective lives. They help to articulate a personal sense of purpose, identify destinations, clarify beliefs and enable the mature person to emerge. The lack of such dialogues can only serve to inhibit aspiration and ambition and so compromise hope. Children's play is often an extended and rich form of utopian dialogue, as alternative worlds are created and explored. The process of such play is as important as the focus of the play – it is about learning how to be hopeful. We cannot help children to be moral and spiritual beings, in their own right, if they do not have the ability to envisage a better world and have a strong sense of what they might become in intellectual, social, moral and spiritual terms:

> Here we connect up with another inescapable feature of human life. I have been arguing that in order to make minimal sense of our lives, in order, to have an identity, we need an orientation to the good, which means some sense of qualitative discrimination, of the incomparably higher. Now we see that this sense of the good has to be woven into my understanding of my life as an unfolding story. But this is to state another basic condition of making sense of ourselves, that we grasp our lives in a *narrative* ... In order to have a sense of who we are, we have to have a notion of how we have become, and of where we are going. (Taylor, 1989, page 47)

Taylor's concept of the 'incomparably higher' is rooted in the centrality of hope. The narrative he describes is the conversation by which hope is located in every life.

The lack of such dialogues might result in both an inability to picture a future and the means to talk about it. Such a state might be described as hopelessness. It is difficult to countenance any circumstances where any person, let alone a child, is in a state of hopelessness. Hope might be perceived as a driving force that integrates all the various dimensions of personal growth. Hope is life enhancing because it provides the sense of purpose that motivates and creates a sense of identity and belonging. It is no coincidence that for many aboriginal peoples dreaming is a cornerstone of their lives as communities and individuals. For Australian aboriginals, the 'Dreaming' refers to all that is known and all that is understood – it determines their relationships with every living creature and every feature of the landscape. Dreaming creates a sense of personal, social and spiritual identity. Growing up in an aboriginal society is a process of gaining understanding of personal dreaming and how it is expressed through dancing, singing, art and the rhythms of everyday life. Hope might be best understood as a type of dreaming – how individuals express their own destiny and their place in the world.

To counteract any sense of hopelessness in children and young people, schools have to become communities of hope. Not in any artificial sense of false expectations denying the reality of people's lives, but rather in the sense of focusing on that which is possible and being affirmative rather than cautiously analytic about the futures of children.

Such an approach might include:

- Regular opportunities for utopian dialogues between adults and children and between children.

- Using narratives of hope, for example biographies and historical accounts.
- Focusing circle time activities on affirmation and reinforcement.
- Celebrating dreams and ambitions.

One strategy that is increasingly being used in many organizations and communities is the concept of appreciative enquiry which works on the basis of positive affirmation rather than a negative, problem-based approach. Appreciative enquiry works on a cyclical approach, as shown in Figure 10.1.

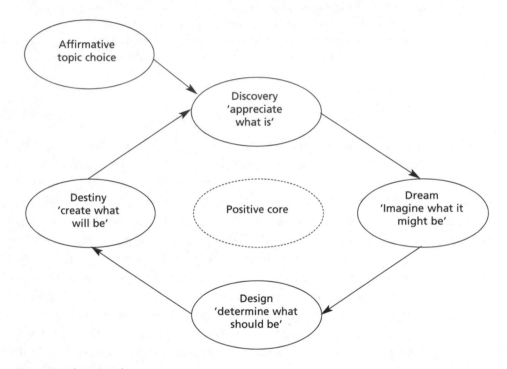

Figure 10.1 The 4-D cycle

The positive core is that which is known to be successful, and serves as the basis for optimism and hope for the future. Affirmative topics are the subjects of strategic importance to the organization, community or person. They may be an aspect of the positive core that, if expanded, would further success. They may be a problem that if stated in the affirmative and studied would improve effectiveness, learning or performance. Or, they may be a success factor that needs to be learned about in order to grow and change. The process works through the following stages.

Discovery – appreciate what is.

This is an extensive, cooperative search to understand the 'best of what is' and 'what has been'.

The discovery process results in:

- A rich description or mapping of the organization's positive core.

- Organization-wide sharing of stories of best practices and exemplary actions.

- Enhanced organizational knowledge and collective wisdom.

- The emergence of unplanned changes well before implementation of the remaining phases of the 4-D cycle.

Dream – imagine what might be

An energizing exploration of 'what might be'. This phase is a time for people to collectively explore hopes and dreams for their future, their work, their working relationships, their organization and the world. It is a time to envision possibilities that are big, bold and beyond the boundaries of what has been in the past.

Design – decide what should be

A set of provocative propositions, describing the ideal future or 'what should be'. They expand the image of the future by presenting clear, compelling pictures of how things will be.

Destiny – create what will be

A series of inspired actions that support ongoing learning and innovation or 'what will be'. The destiny phase focuses specifically on personal and organizational commitments and paths forward. In many cases, appreciative enquiry becomes the framework for leadership and ongoing personal and organizational development

Appreciative enquiry offers a strategy for embedding hope into school life and working to build optimism. As a model it can be used for whole school improvement strategies but it can also be used by small groups and individuals as a structured approach to development. What is important is that because it is an affirmative strategy it changes the dominant language and, so, the culture of the school. This will only happen if all leaders in the school, not just those in positions of seniority, realize the importance of the impact of their language and the need to model appropriate behaviour. This applies as much to hope and optimism as any aspect of school life.

11 Beauty and creativity

Engagement with beauty, and creating beauty, is both a moral act – finding goodness – and a spiritual activity – engaging with the highest expression of life. Sadly, in a culture of celebrity and personality, beauty has become associated with very limited images of physical beauty which are formulaic expressions of cultural stereotypes. Children are highly susceptible to the messages about beauty conveyed in the media, and any strategy to develop moral and spiritual awareness needs to challenge both the stereotypical models of what constitutes beauty and the means by which we engage with the beautiful. The image of the model on the catwalk needs to be challenged by the beauty of a mother nursing her baby and the beauty in the serenity of old age.

Equally we need to help children move from beauty as an absolute object – the ideal, the perfect – to beauty as that which delights, enriches, moves and inspires in whatever way it is expressed:

> To find something beautiful is to register the kinship between the object and the most important part of oneself – one's soul. The beauty of a physical object embodies purity, perfection, harmony and order. And these are, precisely, the qualities that the soul strives to attain in itself. So in the beautiful object we see what we should be. But these qualities are more fully realized in beautiful action, in beauty of character or of mind. When we encounter the beauty of another person's mind or personality, we are presented with the real thing – of this, physical beauty is only an analogy, or a pale reflection. So the moral instances are, in fact, more truly beautiful than any physical thing could be. (Armstrong, 2004, page 72)

Engagement with beauty, however manifested, is essential to any idea of education as growth and development. It provides us with a sense of what is possible, of what we might become. For Gardner (2006a) engagement with the arts – as an expression of beauty and active involvement in its creation – is essential to the realization of children's potential:

Involvement with the arts proves one of the best ways in which children can come to know the greatest achievements of which human beings are capable; it is also an excellent avenue to allow them to contribute to their own culture. If children have these opportunities, they will certainly be using their minds to the fullest. At the same time, they may gain those emotional pleasures, those moments of inspiration, and those feeling of mystical involvement which commentators once thought were the special province of the arts. (page 101)

In a later work, Gardner (2006b) links childhood with creativity:

Members of one age group need little pressure to assume the creative stance – young children even before the age of formal schooling. Given even a modestly supportive environment, youngsters are not only intrigued by a wide range of phenomena, experiences, topics, and questions; they persist in exploring, even in the absence of encouragement, let alone material rewards. Few are the children who are not galvanized by a trip to a country fair, an amusement park, or a children's museum; their playfulness, curiosity, and imaginative powers are palpable. The mind of the five-year-old represents, in one sense, the height of creative powers. (page 84)

We celebrate, enable and support creativity because it allows for the possibility of the emergence of something beautiful and, just as importantly, the understanding and confidence to engage with beauty. The difference is listening to a piece of music or looking at a painting and being told that it is beautiful and learning what is involved in creating beauty.

When a doting parent celebrates the free-expression in paint by their three-year-old with the response 'That's beautiful' and fixes it to the fridge door, the possibility of engagement with creativity and beauty is reinforced. Picasso said '… it has taken me my whole life to learn to draw like a child' (cited in Gardner, 2006b, page 84). Involvement in the creation of physical beauty strengthens our capacity to explore, understand and express moral and spiritual beauty.

Craft (2002) provides an important distinction between creativity as manifest in the work of great arts and her concept of 'little c creativity' which she defines as: '… a creativity of everyday life' (page 43).

The notion of little c creativity goes beyond 'doing it differently', 'finding alternative' or 'producing novelty', for it involves having some grasp of the domain of application, and thus of the appropriateness of the ideas. It involves the use of imagination, intelligence, self-creation and self-expression. (ibid., page 45)

Craft goes on to identify the characteristics of creativity-based approaches in the classroom:

- being open to possibility, the unknown and the unexpected
- bridging differences – making connections between apparently unconnected ideas and integrating different ways of knowing (for example, physical, feeling, imagining)
- holding the paradox of form and freedom
- holding the tension between safety and risk
- being willing to give and receive criticism
- awareness of the individual. (*ibid*., page 152)

These characteristics could be applied equally to any model of spiritual and moral development, and reinforce the model of learning for understanding outlined in Chapter 5. Csikszentmihalyi (1997) approaches the same broad theme from a different perspective. He has developed the concept of flow to describe those optimum moments of engagement, involvement, focus, creativity and fulfilment that led to the happiness discussed in Theme 9:

> Self-consciousness disappears, yet one feels stronger than usual. The sense of time is distorted: hours seem to pass by in minutes. When a person's entire being is stretched in the full functioning of body and mind, whatever one does becomes worth doing for its own sake; living becomes its own justification. In the harmonious focusing of physical and psychic energy, life finally comes into its own. (pages 31–2)

It is in this state that optimum performance in sport is likely to be achieved, it is the breakthrough in understanding a mathematical problem, it is when a creative project suddenly comes together – it is about insight and finding new ways forward.

Csikszentmihalyi is very clear that flow is neither the result of a miraculous intervention nor luck. It is rather the interplay between the skills an individual has and an appropriate level of challenge:

> Optimal experiences usually involve a fine balance between ones' ability to act, and the available opportunities for action. (ibid., page 30)

If the balance is not right, then the alternative states, shown in Figure 11.1, will prevail.

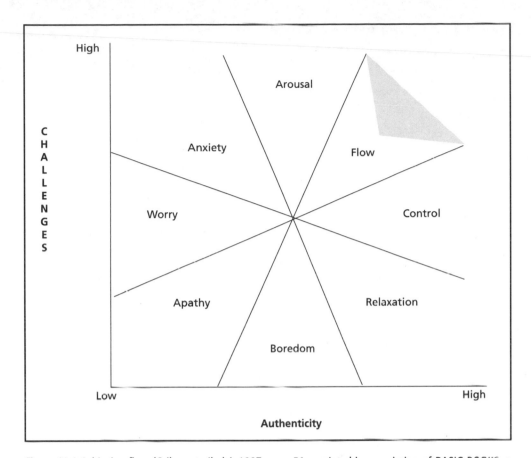

Figure 11.1 Achieving flow (Csikszentmihalyi, 1997, page 31, reprinted by permission of BASIC BOOKS, a member of Perseus Books Group)

The role of the teacher is to maximize the possibilities of flow by identifying optimal challenges and ensuring that the relevant skills are available. The discussion of reflection and stillness is an example of how the circumstances can be created, which will allow the possibility of flow. Once flow has been experienced then it becomes much easier to have conversation about beauty and creativity because flow ensures that the experience is both personal and authentic. Flow, creative thinking and the ability to be confident about moral and spiritual experiences will be supported by strategies that include:

• questioning and challenging
• making connections and seeing relationships
• speculating and proposing
• developing options

- generating alternative modes of expression
- ability to visualize ideas
- flexible and adaptable thinking
- creating new knowledge by making connections
- involvement in creative projects
- analysing and understanding various manifestations of beauty
- reflection and internalization.

The skills that will support flow and give confidence in approaching tasks involving creativity could include:

1. Five 'hows' and five 'whys'
2. Brainstorming
3. Mind mapping
4. Opposites and contradictions
5. Free talk ('What if …', 'Why not …')
6. Random association
7. Plead ignorance
8. Naive logic
9. Divergent and convergent thinking
10. Green hat thinking (de Bono)
11. Insight and intuition

For creativity to flourish, the school, classroom and all learning environments will need most of the following characteristics:

- Teachers as facilitators, co-constructors of knowledge, questions not answers
- High emotional security – high challenge–low risk
- Pupil choice and negotiation
- Review and reflection
- Cognitive toolkit – thinking skills
- Celebration, affirmation and reinforcement
- Time to think, create and learn
- Assessment-shared success criteria
- Direct experience, experiential learning, doing not listening
- Working with creative people – poets, artists, musicians and engineers.

Learners who are actively engaged in being creative will be better able to understand value and respond to the creativity of others. Direct personal experience of creativity will enable a more thoughtful engagement with the many manifestations of beauty. This in turn will encourage and support spiritual growth, which in turn fosters moral confidence:

> … creativity goes hand in glove with disciplinary thinking. In the absence of relevant disciplines, it is not possible to be genuinely creative. In the absence of creativity, disciplines can be used only to rehearse the status quo. Moreover, creativity itself has different facets. The personality of the creative individual – robust, risk taking, resilient needs to be cultivated from early on … (Gardner, 2006b, page 162)

12 Reflection and stillness

The ability to reflect and the positive enjoyment of stillness and silence are essential to learning to engage with the spiritual. All of the great faiths stress the centrality of reflection, silence and stillness – often under the broad heading of meditation. This is clearly counter to a world of seemingly non-stop noise and stimulation. The constant availability of music, cartoons, computer games, television programmes and text messages means that many children are in a permanent state of engagement with external stimuli. There are few opportunities for silence, and silence may actually become intimidating. Equally, the introspection that reflection requires will be difficult for many who are permanently focused on the external. This is why the focus on the natural world, discussed in Theme 8, is so important.

Any approach to moral and spiritual development that seeks to create authentic, personal responses has to engage with reflection and stillness. It might be appropriate to see these as skills or behaviours that have to be learned in order to facilitate the development of the other attributes discussed in this section of the book. Of course, there are very real problems in introducing reflection to children. Apart from their 'busy' environments, they may well lack the ability to concentrate for long periods and find it difficult to focus on one topic for any length of time – in fairness, many adults also have these problems. Equally, reflection involves a high level of engagement with abstract and conceptual thinking.

There are numerous strategies to support reflection, but two seem particularly appropriate as they involve 'mental action'. The first involves selecting a theme, say kindness, and then asking children to imagine they are going on a journey and to reflect on practical examples of kindness that they might see, be the beneficiary of, or actually do for others. At first the teacher may provide the narrative for the journey, as well as scenarios which will encourage the development of examples through building scenarios; for example:

- A child lost in an airport.
- Coming across a minor traffic accident.
- Somebody who has lost their entire luggage.
- Waiting because of a delayed flight.
- A lost tourist with poor English.

The second strategy is based around utopian scenario building, 'In a perfect world …'. Children might be asked to create a vision of a village or neighbourhood where a range of qualities are found, for example fairness, equity and inclusion, and then explore the practical manifestations of everyday life.

It is important to stress that reflection is not necessarily about silence. Silence is an important element but sharing, explaining and clarifying are equally important components. The outcomes of any reflection need to be articulated and consolidated. Equally, reflection does not have to be over-solemn or portentous.

It can be quick-fire to catch a significant moment in the classroom or to respond to an important event. What is vital is that reflection is built into the life of the classroom so that it becomes a natural and essential component of daily routines. White (2000) describes in detail the approach she developed:

> There are a number of suitable times when reflection could be entered into for the first time. I have found it works best at the end of a wet or windy playtime or at the end of a hectic day. It is also an interesting way to begin a religious education lesson. I have also used reflection time as an introduction to a discussion about an important issue or before debating rules for classroom behaviour. (page 20)

> Guaranteeing, as far as possible, that there are no interruptions to your reflection time is essential. It is important that the group is not disturbed or distracted as this could lead to a devaluation of the whole experience. It is also important that the room is made as dark as possible, perhaps closing blinds or drawing the curtains to windows or to the quiet area. (page 21)

> Any calm and quiet music would be suitable for an initial experience, although a group will usually choose and identify any favourites. Different types of music work for different groups. It is relevant to allow children to listen to a wide range of music in order to develop their critical skills (page 21).

> In my experience a large candle is more effective for reflection time. In our classroom the candle is usually placed on a plate, which is then placed on another object, which raises it higher than eye level. I use an upturned plastic box covered with a patterned cloth, which is placed on our 'special' rug. (page 22)

The time it takes to conduct a reflection time varies; it may take about 10 minutes or longer, although to begin with it is probably advisable to keep it short, extending it as the group becomes more used to it. The ending of a piece of music usually indicates a natural finishing point. (page 22)

Through the use of these tools I wanted to create a space and a calm time within which children would be left alone, not physically of course, but alone in the sense of nothing being directly asked of them other than to sit and to listen. (page 5)

After the session, children may choose to discuss the activity or what they were thinking about or they may choose to keep their thoughts private. Respecting this choice is all part of the process. The children often enjoy the power of being able to say, 'My thoughts are private'. (page 22)

Linda White's (2000) model combines a range of strategies to create an optimum situation to support calm introspection as a prelude to a circle time strategy. The comments of her class clearly indicate this approach:

'I like when the candle's on because you can think about anything and you can think about different countries and the people who haven't got any toys. I'm looking for things I can give away to other people who haven't got any toys. Sometimes when the candle's on I think about my mum and my teacher.' Chloe (page 23)

'When you do reflection you've got a picture in your head you have to colour and you've forgot what to do, when you do reflection again you can think of that picture again.' Kevin (page 23)

'It gives you peace.' Callum (page 25)

'It's like when you look at the sun, when you close your eyes it's like the light comes through to you. It's resting when you are in a mess. It makes you calm and quiet again. When you've been scrappy, it makes you more calm.' Trevor (page 26)

Reflection is a central strategy in the development of self-awareness and increasing confidence in approaching complex issues of spiritual and moral development. Reflection makes the abstract concrete and the generic personal. It can be found in many situations and it is for the adults in school to take the opportunity, for example 'At the end of a dance lesson with year 2 pupils as the music faded we held the moment and held the pose for a few seconds. We then relaxed and smiled with such understanding and then later reflected how we had felt, described our feelings and then explored other occasions when we had felt like that.'

A residential escape, especially somewhere like Holy Island, provides a range of opportunities for stillness if this is seen as a part of the total social and learning experience.

13 Death and loss

Death raises profound moral and spiritual questions – in many ways it is pivotal to the most fundamental questions about the purpose and nature of life. Engagement with topics related to death and loss focus our thinking on elemental themes:

• Why do we have to die?

• Whose fault is the death of a loved one?

• How do we come to terms with grief and loss?

• What happens after death?

• What does death tell us about life?

As a society we have come a long way from the routine inevitability of death, especially of children, of several hundred years ago. Equally, we have moved beyond the morbid Victorian celebration of death and the related denial of death as an inevitable part of life. Children who watch television programmes will be exposed to multiple manifestations of death – from the denial of natural laws found in cartoons to the almost casual images found in television dramas to the sanitized reality of news programmes – many of which deny the real suffering and death which still exist for many adults and children around the world, caused by famine, disease and conflict. A substantial proportion of the most popular computer games centre on the ability to 'kill' opponents and having killed them know that they will return when the game is next played.

In a recent review of the film 'Final Destination 3' by Catterall (2007) these casual images are reinforced:

> Another outing for this blackly-comic franchise, containing the most gleefully inventive movie deaths since Dr Phibes and the *Saw* series. High school clairvoyant Wendy rescues her pals from death-by-rollercoaster, but a short-changed Grim Reaper (as much a

character in its own right as the doomed jocks and teen queens), insists on cashing in. Cue death by tanning ('It's way too warm in here, huh'), nail-gun, and re-enactment society. As with *Casualty*, half the fun's in second-guessing which accidental combination of household objects will prove fatal. (page 65)

Except in tragic circumstances modern cultural expectations distance us from death, or rather from dying. Thus death and dying are trivialized and made banal, death is desensitized which has implications for our ability to engage meaningfully, show compassion and respond to injustice and inequality.

Death, as a state, is often confused with dying as a process. Dying potentially involves pain and culminates in the modern bureaucracy of death and its associated rituals. Often the fear of death is actually the fear of dying and the related emotional responses of those seeing a loved one suffer. Grief is an expression of loss – the level of grief a reflection of the depth of love. The vicarious suffering caused by the pain of another and the anticipation of loss is one of the highest expressions of empathy. As such it is very difficult for children to come to terms with. Children have complex emotional responses to death which are closely linked to emotional and cognitive development. It is possible to identify four, very broad, stages of the development of understanding about death:

1. Very young children are unable to conceptualize death as a permanent state – there may be an expectation that the dead person will return.

2. Early years children will often see death as reversible and not realize that life and death are mutually exclusive. They may also attribute the death of a relative to their own behaviour.

3. Primary age children will recognize the inevitability of death and that it is a permanent state. They recognize the mortality of all living things and may express a morbid (to adults) interest in the physical details of dying and death.

4. Adolescents have the ability to conceptualize death and adopt their family and community norms, beliefs and practices associated with death.

Irrespective of age or emotional and cognitive development death will generate a wide range of emotional responses which may well be emulated by children. Fear, anger, sadness, loss and guilt will be expressed in varying degrees and various permutations according to the specific circumstances:

The fundamental question is how to deal with others' deaths. We grieve the loss of an element in what made our world meaningful. There is an unavoidable process of healing – of making whole – to be endured, marked in many societies by formal periods of mourning, between one and three years long. But the world is never again entire after bereavement. We do not get over losses; we merely learn to live with them.

There is a great consolation. Two facts – that the dead once lived; and that one loved them and mourned their loss – are inexpugnably part of the world's history. So the presence of those who lived can never be removed from time, which is to say that there is a kind of eternity after all. (Grayling, 2001, pages 31–2)

One of the problems in dealing with death in schools is that childhood is normally, hopefully, focused on life-affirming activities – the language of families, classrooms and schools is positive, optimistic, forward looking and full of hope. It seems almost cruel to introduce death into this equation. And yet, death is a factor in school life, whether the impact of a family bereavement on a child, the death of a member of the school community or, most tragically the death of a child. This situation is compounded by the circumstances of death. The peaceful, dignified and anticipated death of a grandparent is very different to the violent death of a child. Clearly, any form of religious education will focus on the particular beliefs about what happens after death. The ubiquitous concept of heaven does, for many, provide hope and reassurance and helps to contextualize death. However, such beliefs are not within the remit of this study. What follows can be adapted to fit the needs of any faith or lack of faith.

Many aspects of spiritual development focus on dying and death. Awareness and experience of death will clarify many of the previous themes in this section and the ability to come to terms with grief and loss are essential components of personal growth and authenticity.

It could be argued that one of the best reasons for having family pets is that their life-span is usually short. For many children the first experience of death is a goldfish or hamster. One of the advantages of having small rodents in classrooms is the learning opportunities occasioned by their demise. What is important is to help children develop a vocabulary and a portfolio of strategies to come to terms with dying and death.

Kübler-Ross and Kessler (2005) offer a five-stage model of grief and loss, as follows:

Denial is the first stage, the refusal to accept the reality of loss, questioning and challenging and then gradually coming to terms with the reality of loss. Young children in particular may be in very strong denial simply because they will be unable to conceptualize a world without the person who has died.

Denial may lead into the second stage – anger. Children may demonstrate anger at the dead person for abandoning them, at doctors and nurses for failing to save them, at other adults for not preparing them and, most worryingly, at themselves. Anger may also be directed at God – whatever its source, anger is an expression of pain, a sense of abandonment and unfairness.

Alongside anger, or following it, is bargaining, often the product of guilt. Bargaining may be expressed as a 'deal with God', an internal debate about 'what ifs' and 'if only'. In essence, this stage is about achieving understanding.

When the reality of death is accepted then the fourth stage may emerge – depression.

Depression can be seen as a negative to be avoided by whatever means available or a cathartic process of adjustment – moving from desperate grief into sadness and so into the final stage – acceptance.

Acceptance is the process of reordering the world, adjusting and realigning the way in which the rhythms and patterns of life have changed. Acceptance allows us to grow – to continue the spiritual journey:

> Finding acceptance may be just having more good days than bad. As we begin to live again and enjoy our life, we often feel that in doing so, we are betraying our loved one. We can never replace what has been lost, but we can make new connections, new meaningful relationships, new interdependencies. Instead of denying our feelings, we listen to our needs; we move, we change, we grow, we evolve. We may start to reach out to others and become involved in their lives. We invest in our friendships and in our relationship with ourself. We begin to live again, but we cannot do so until we have given grief its time.
> (Kübler-Ross and Kessler, 2005, page 28)

All of the above points help to identify some principles for conversations with children about dying and death:

1. Be as objective and factual as possible.
2. Avoid euphemisms: 'He's gone to sleep' means that he will wake up.
3. Deal with the immediate reality by recognizing fear and uncertainty rather than pretending nothing has really changed.
4. It may be helpful to stress:
   - that death cannot be prevented;
   - that dying does not mean the end of loving;
   - that death is not a punishment for those left;
   - that the dead person will never come back;
   - it is OK to feel worried, bewildered, scared, sad and angry;
   - it is important to eat, sleep, play and do all the normal things.

These principles can be applied in dialogue with an individual child or as the basis for a circle time discussion following the widely reported death of a public figure, the pet of one of the class or (as and when appropriate) the bereavement of one of the class or the teacher.

It might also be appropriate to explore the rituals associated with death – notably funerals. Issues around interment and cremation may need to be explored, as will forms of service and the language used.

Spirituality is defined and bounded by mortlity. Perhaps the greatest insight that children can be offered is the opportunity to celebrate life, to learn through loss and to be supported in developing their own sense of self. For significant numbers of children the possibility of death is all too real; those who live with drug-dependent parents and carers; those beaten on a regular basis; those told by parents and carers that their lives would be better if the child was dead. The traumatization that this can lead to denies the possibility of spiritual growth and raises the spectre of a cycle of denial and impoverishment being passed on to another generation. Openness and confidence in these issues becomes essential in the school.

14 Celebrating the transcendent

It may just be a coincidence, but have you noticed that the components of a romantic evening out – candles, flowers, music, food, a special place and distinctive clothes – bear an uncanny resemblance to the liturgy of the world's religions? As human beings we have a very limited imagination when it comes to celebrating the significant events in our lives. Across time and cultures the essential elements remain the same. What vary, of course, are the motivation for and the object of the celebration.

Any understanding of spiritual development has to recognize the importance and centrality of celebration. For most faiths this is usually described as worship and almost always involves some form of liturgy. The coming together of people for a common purpose to engage in a shared ritual is found in almost every community. Military units, football supporters, members of fox hunts, politicians and numerous other groups are drawn to some form of collective activity to celebrate their identity and to find inspiration, comfort and reassurance from being together with a common purpose and shared activities. Whether it's the Trooping of the Colour parade, or a sing-song in the coach after a football match, there is an engagement with the intangible, the elusive sense of community that meets both emotional and social needs. The numerous manifestations of tribal rituals around the world are clearly designed to celebrate and reinforce a sense of shared identity. Schools recognize this too and have traditions and celebrations to enhance a sense of belonging and celebrate a shared identity and a sense of being together. Many celebrations have a cyclical nature, across the year or seasons or each day – for example the metronomic prayer life of the monastery. However, there has to be opportunity for the spontaneous celebration and the capturing of unanticipated moments of significance and value.

Hick (1999) argues that all of the above expressions (to varying degrees) are manifestations of what he calls the 'fifth dimension'. This is the sense that there is something more than the base physicality of our lives. This is the dimension that explains the sense of wonder in the astronomer contemplating the galaxies and the neuroscientist explaining the deepest recesses of the brain. It is the feeling of exhilaration in performing a piece of music, in watching a sunset, in seeing animals in the wild for the first time, in the unconditional love for another. It may also be found in the delight of marching in step, chanting on the terraces, holding a new-born lamb and watching chicks hatching. It is found in the high mass and in reading poetry and playing with children. As Hick (1999) recognizes, we have problems in talking about this aspect of our lives:

> The fifth dimension of our nature, the transcendent within us, answers to the fifth dimension of the universe, the transcendent without. In speaking of this, the limitations of language create a problem to which there is unfortunately no satisfactory solution … Absolute Reality, the Real, the Transcendent, the Divine, the Holy, the Eternal, the Infinite – with or without capitals … It is now allusive, suggestive, metaphorical, poetic, pointing rather than defining. And so we have continually to try to focus, not on the pointing finger of language, but on that to which it points. (pages 8–9)

The title of this theme, 'celebrating the transcendent', is an attempt to move away from the inherited cultural connotations that go with worship. Our argument is that the form and object of such celebration is less important than the fact that it is available and engaged in, to allow for the full expression of our shared humanity. Central to most forms of celebration is the notion of giving thanks for that which we have and share. Recognizing what is already in our lives, rather than asking for more, and reinforcing and consolidating that which is good and significant.

Language is often inadequate in this context, but all of the experiences outlined so far in these themes move people to use words and phrases such as: sublime, awe, mystery, wonder. This is why music, dance and ritual become so important – they enable the expression of feelings when words are inadequate. One of the reasons that we come together to celebrate transcendence is that the collective act actually reinforces and intensifies the feelings and enables us to explore them with confidence and security. Celebrating transcendence through shared rituals in communities nourishes and sustains and enhances the potential for personal and collective growth and learning, and provides opportunities for shared pleasure and enjoyment.

Celebrating the transcendent can take many forms:

- Prayer – collective acts expressing hope, gratitude, supplication and affirmation.
- Sacrifice – offerings made in gratitude or appeasement.
- Rituals – ceremonies that are invested with significance and status.
- Festivals – public celebrations focused on particular themes.
- Pilgrimages – journeys that involve aspects of the other elements in this list.
- Music-making and listening to significant music: from hymns to the last night of the Proms.

- Dance – covering the full range of kinaesthetic and aesthetic expression.

- Contemplation and meditation – shared stillness and silence.

- Special places – churches, mosques, temples, synagogues, spaces in nature, Stonehenge, football terraces, the home.

- Language – forms of service, sermons, poetry, stories, narratives and drama.

All of the above, and the endless permutations they offer, provide ways of celebrating the transcendent that are appropriate to time, place and culture. What is important is that there are multiple opportunities to celebrate the transcendent in as many different ways as there are expressions of spirituality. Thus, there is the need for the whole school assembly with music, poetry and dance to celebrate and reinforce shared beliefs and common identity. There is also the need for the quiet corner of the garden for personal reflection or shared understanding. But it is also important to enable joy and celebration in lessons, to encourage and support reflection and, crucially, to enable rich and meaningful dialogue so that understanding is achieved, consolidated and celebrated.

> The heart of learning is returning always to the heart of all life. The heart of life is openness, awareness, and wholeness inseparable. It is the Great Chain of Being: the joining of form and the formless, the joining of matter and spirit, the joining of sacred and profane. The heart of leaning is learning to see ourselves and this living world as totally, utterly, and completely inseparable – as whole. The heart of learning is, finally, learning from and attending to the life thread of spirit pervading and connecting all things. (Glazer, 1999, page 250)

Part 3

Case Study

Case study – Vanessa Huws Jones

Introduction

Have you ever watched 'The Apprentice'– well, the first series any way – the one that had sparkle and intrigue and that 'can't wait for the next instalment' factor? I liked Saira, she came second. She was gutsy, said what she thought and really stuck to her principles, especially when challenged and particularly when held to account. She was good and knew she was, yet she always gave one the impression that she wanted to learn and find out more in order to better herself and, therefore, those and the organization around her. She engaged at a deep level and her relationships, although tricky sometimes, were authentic and genuine, and never selfish. I liked her.

Not strange then to read an article about her in a Sunday newspaper recently, where she was promoting her book – all about goal setting and how important it is to gaining a successful and happy life. Is it? Surely there is so much more as well? Yes, Saira says there is and, here is the nub, your goals should be based around those core values that you hold dear.

So what are my core values and what have they got to do with this case study? Where and when did they come from? Now? Ten years ago as I entered headship? Sixteen years ago when I entered the teaching profession? Or perhaps always – since the day I began to articulate and make sense of the world from those early years as a child. How have I articulated them through my vocation, or should I say through my professional relationships? This is an attempt to share with you how I obtained my core values. The story is not unique but I do believe it is special. It is not about me but about the powerful expression of those relationships I have engaged in with children and adults – all learners – how we all interacted socially, morally and spiritually during the past six years and all that has been entailed.

Are we discussing my core values or my moral drivers?

I like the following six keywords: integrity, authenticity, quality, trust, hope, oh and love. There is a lot to think about. Could I – have I – determined my goals, my vision and my mission through these values? Yes, and through relationships, relationships,

relationships. My mentor gave me the Michael Fullan book *Leading in a Culture of Change* (2001) to read after my most testing early years and I sort of wish I'd had it before I started. Or do I? It is quite nice to see how one's practice has been echoed with the theory. The book was all about leading in a culture of change. And when I now reflect back, I'm not sure that I was intrinsically aware that, when I became a headteacher, I was beginning to build a moral and spiritual community or, indeed, as time went on, that the team – the members of staff – thought that either. We certainly started with aiming to establish an effective and efficient organization and the key characteristics were there – vertical communication top down and bottom up, as you will see later, but it was only when the relationships – people becoming people through people – blossomed that we exchanged and then emerged from transactions to transformation. I remember how three members of staff lost their parents in the last year that we were all together and yet they all came to 'their second family home for love and support'. Love was largely present in our community, especially in the latter years. We talked about loving each other in our special way and it was the accepted and only way for us all to be. I felt that our community had real soul.

'The people are not separate here, they are family.' (Tom, Year 3)

All of us enjoyed continuing to explore and to create within our vocations. We were confident about what we were individually and together and we valued what we had.

I do believe that, being the privileged educators of children that we are, we do need to grasp this concept and really run with it. There is so much excellent practice out there and so much more we can do for our communities' spiritual and moral growth if only we were able to recognize what we are doing already. Our school communities do have a shared meaning and purpose – indeed we have to articulate that clearly now on Ofsted documents – and those truly outstanding schools are full of human beings of whatever age who are able, expected, supported and mentored to realize their full humanity, and they do that through a rich network of relationships within and through the school community. So perhaps through reading this case study, and recognizing so much of it, I'm sure, in your own context you will begin to gain a deeper understanding, faith and hold of what it is to lead and be part of a spiritual and moral community.

The early days and people (trust)

We talked about change a lot. I did, discussing the original vision with the governors – a robust, strong group of people, who were very clear about what they wanted and incredibly supportive – but even they did not realize just how fragmented the organization was underneath: cans of worms and all that. I am not sure some of them believed me either at first. A member of staff called Jane commented, 'The appointment of a new headteacher was pivotal: she inherited a school which had many very good staff who worked hard but felt undervalued; where teamwork and mutual support were patchy and where the climate was one of sticking to what was being done well, with no risk taking.'

The staff – all of them – also talked about the desire for change. Twenty-five years under the same headteacher had been a long time. I interviewed – very informally – all of them in the May prior to my September start. Another member of the staff recalls, 'She consulted all staff individually about their perceptions of their role in school and how she could facilitate them to carry it out more effectively.'

Some of the staff came in groups – the midday supervisors (their elected leader, even though they did not want one or officially had one) told me quite categorically that all was well and they were fine, and that the previous head had been absolutely fine with everything at lunchtimes – 'hadn't he girls!' That was not what subsequent questionnaires and chats with children said.

And then there was the admin officer. She was crying out for support in her role and so wanted to move out of the broom cupboard she had for an office, which had no proper light! And then there were some of the younger staff, whose potential and spark were slowly diminishing as the encouragement and support reservoir was near empty. One can only be self-sufficient for so long.

And then the deputy who said she was *really* looking forward to me coming but yet that 'blink' moment made me question the truth. And the assistant head who eyed me so suspiciously and answered every question with a question, and I knew I was going to be tested to see what I was made from. I had to earn my stripes and prove my worth.

They were lovely, lovely people but they were not a team. And they did, quite reasonably, want to be appreciated, they did want to understand and they did want to feel 'in' on things. I began to suspect that I had three groups. There were those who I knew would be casualties on the way, those who would stick at it and tell me in no uncertain terms when I had gone too far too soon but still hold on, and those who would be with me every step of the way and quietly stay with me through thick and thin. I didn't know which groups they would fall in to but I had a fair idea. And where, as I reflect still further and encourage you to do the same, does that sense come from? Do we instinctively derive from deep within us as knowing it is right? Some of the staff did surprise me – what a delight – and of course some of them behaved just as predicted. One of my teaching assistants – a very wise and emotionally intelligent lady – commented later, 'the leadership skills of the head were crucial as she sensitively but very firmly led the school in this climate of change: it was never going to be easy coaxing people out of their comfort zones'. It sometimes felt too much like the task versus relationships dilemma.

Parents were a joy – so ready for change – and they did not expect much. I felt angry that they had been content with so little for so long. I wanted to show then just what it could be like and what they deserved for their children. They were entitled to better and I wanted to repay them for their patience and lack of interference as they allowed me to get on with the job. I'd had parental interference – not interest – before and that really impedes progress.

The children were bright, positive, energetic and full of potential. They were mighty special in fact, and so ready and ripe for what was to come. And they delivered and delivered and kept delivering.

> 'Everyone gets a chance here and we're pleased for them. We get all the chance we need.'
> (Alice, Year 5)

I do believe that one of the skills I tried hard with was encouraging them to trust me – trust is pivotal. It is so hard to build up and yet, as we all know, so easy to destroy. They had to trust me in those early days and, in true organizational fashion, I worked with a style of power and consent that you will see as you read on. We used our assembly/coming together time as our opportunity to be explicit about what we wanted to become. We developed small but significant habits and routines. I modelled, they modelled and folk followed. Our early years, as you will see later when we unpick the vision, were about policies and procedures and roles. These led to our own set of principles that became apparent in time through our shared behaviours, and vocabulary that we continually went back to, evaluated and often renewed. I used the performance management vehicle as such a powerful tool here to enable parts of this structure building to hold secure those early fragile foundations.

The key driver was very simple yet quite complex. Was what I wanted to provide in our school good enough for my own children? There were no children of my own but that was irrelevant. Was every single aspect of the school's life and community going to be good enough? That means *everything*. Every conversation, every engagement/encounter, every lesson, every assembly, every raw material they ever used to learn with, and every resource – with our most powerful resource being people.

I do believe that it is true dialogue in which people engage with each other, not to control but to provoke and be provoked, to learn and contribute to the learning of others, to challenge their own minds as well as the minds of others.

As our journey went on, I think we learned that people adapt more successfully to their environment, given their purposes and values, by facing painful circumstances and developing new attitudes and behaviours. They learn to live with things that cannot be changed and take responsibility for those they can.

Quite simply, we learned to interact and participate together and one of the most privileged aspects of the last six years has been seeing that happen in a variety of ways, with most of the now strong and empowered teams of amazing people. The flip-side of that coin is the challenge aspect of the last six years. I think it has been where I have had to force, at times, the issue about taking responsibility.

'All of a sudden you find yourself in year six and THAT is a responsibility to others.'
(Jasmine, Year 6)

Responsibility is about participating. There is a wonderful section in *Fantastic Mr Fox* by Roald Dahl where, after having had his tail shot at once, he attempts to come out of his hole again. He contemplates the night air and then goes through a ritual of shuffles and sniffs until he feels safe enough to expose his whole body and then he is off, on his mission with a task in hand. I think participation in a new organization is like that in the early stages but, when one does get going, the sense of empowerment and self-esteem is tremendous. It is not by sheer luck that, as time went on, members of the school community emerged from roles such as helping mums to advanced teaching assistants, midday supervisor to learning mentor, advanced teaching assistants to teacher. It is not by coincidence that the original, fragmented, dependant group became, in time, the independent team who then later flourished to become an interdependent community.

We were all just friends initially. We liked each other (most of the time), but in time that changed. We started to actually enjoy being together and that in turn led to, what I certainly considered, to be a loving community: the kind of loving community that you can lean on and take comfort from in hard times. Times when one knows that the decisions you are about to make will *change* people, their lives and their family's lives for ever. Times when one knows that those decisions could potentially be quite *damaging* for that person, their lives and families, and indeed their view of the world. Times when one knows that's what you *have* to do because those children deserve better and because they get *one* chance and because we have been entrusted with their potential.

'We are nice ... and happy and it passes on. You take it into somebody like a good book and it can go on for ever.' (Mikey, Year 3)

The dialogue we shared (beliefs and values)

I shared my vision, which had got me the job in the first place, with the staff. They were very thrilled with that idea of sharing and being involved, and we did it sat on tiny chairs in the reception class where it all begins. It was the first of many pivotal conversations: 'We knew after that that you would value us and were interested in what we had to say.' And afterwards we all talked about it and wrote down how we felt. Actually, we wrote down how we felt, what we had done and what the impact was: quite a lot during the first four years. It was massively important. They all expected it and I could see with my slowly forming senior management team (note: management team) just where we were, how they were thinking and whether we were on the right track.

The original vision was very practical and contained all the basic elements necessary for good effective school improvement – it wasn't rocket science. But it was concrete and measurable and involved talking together about teaching and attainment and was quite prescriptive and 'top down' and very focused in management outcomes. We had to see tangible things that told us we were doing well and that all was fine - for the time being. The organization was rudderless and fragmented. They screamed out for leadership, the firm, focused and effective leadership style that would tell, show and guide. My style was one of coercing and coaching, said the Leadership Programme for Serving Headteachers (LPSH) data at the end of the first year! That was a shock at first when I read that of myself, but how appropriate in those early stages and how necessary to build those strong foundations and then for others to model themselves as subsequent smaller sub-teams formed as the years went on.

The role of the headteacher was a crucial part of the vision, a role I didn't fully appreciate in the context of the community's expectations and interesting now to reflect on under the possible cameos of the extended school community.

I was concerned about so much yet it did not worry me. The local authority took a similar view but supported me consistently on many levels for a good long while. 'This school should be a flagship for the authority,' said one of the principal advisers, 'you need to make it one!'

There was not a real School Development Plan. There was in a fashion but not one that anyone knew about or was in operation. It was not linked to the budget and therefore the potential for creativity was huge. Quite a novelty to actually share how to write one with staff and give them their own budget and ask them to decide what their subject needed. We did talk about coordinating the subjects at that stage, not leading them, and it did 'hurt' to allow a day's supply to 'sort out the cupboard, please' but I had to – they had to – and then and only then could we move on. It just seemed there was little real overarching sense or order to so much of what I inherited. Why were Year 2 children in a class next to Year 6? Why had some of the staff been in the same classroom and year group for ten years?

Within six weeks we (the governors and I) had rearranged ten classes into 11 and had some minor building work done. Bit of a risk so early, but isn't the greatest hazard in life to risk nothing?

And this was about entitlement that our children should have had. It meant smaller classes and therefore a greater potential for quality teaching and learning. We had started to make the vision a reality.

There were some things that just did not occur to me. Surely there were job descriptions? Surely not – how I misread that one big time. 'I'm not doing all this', said one member or staff. 'I was only asked to do this because there was no one else and I'd attended a case study on it.' A teacher coordinating health and safety – that was novel – again too much too soon, gosh I learned so much in those first two terms. They were so willing to move on but not at my pace and who could blame them really. I was frustrated but I had to slow down. They told me nicely. I listened. We all took time to breathe slowly. We prepared job descriptions and did them in the context of performance management. It was a government initiative that really helped – once I had showed them it would help them. Once I had shown them that it was about *them* – valuing and investing in them. Yes, I did want to come and spend time with them in their classrooms – spend time, not observe or monitor – goodness what had happened to these talented folk to dread that so much? We chose quality teaching and learning as the first things to focus on. We talked about the criteria that I gave them. We used simple and straightforward statements, and planned the timetable very carefully with allotted feedback times where we had one to one and with me – only me – time. The findings from the feedback were collated and fed back to everyone, moving on slowly to repeat the whole exercise all over again the next term. It was made explicit that this was going to happen next term, and the one after that, and the one after that, and soon we would move away from just me as leader and look at other staff to lead. But who? It had to be someone who had earned their stripes and had credibility and it wasn't someone in my current senior team.

My key stage coordinator worked hard with me to get this next stage right – she lacked confidence at first and I was unsure why. She was good. I modelled, she followed and it became a success. My first delegated leadership move. It didn't go much further at the time but I had sussed the potential, I think we both had. She really took some convincing but eventually three years later she did apply to lead an internal team and is stunning in the position. One of the very best – I learned a lot from her.

We moved to team and subject *leadership* much later, but we did do it. It was a journey and a process, and the early formative stages had to be done. Seemed strange to be looking at quality teaching and learning when we didn't really have schemes of work. Against my better judgement we adopted initially the QCA units. Looking back now it gave us a good content-driven curriculum, which I think many found was appropriate at the time. We had to have a structure that would unite us and give us some consistency where we could team around common themes. We pulled it all apart years later but at the time it was essential. I have worried since at how it may have deskilled some of my better staff and lost some of that creativity, but prescriptive, tangible, outcome-focused direction was what was needed. We used it, just as we did performance management, to align and create some shape.

We did the same with policies as well. There were some documents, but they were not shared and were kept in box, and some of the most obvious ones were just not there. Assessment was one example, and how shocked the local authority was, two months in, when I explained how difficult it was to target set when we had no assessment procedures in the school. And what other policies were missing as well? Why was a senior teacher out of class during lesson time, getting something out of a cupboard in the staffroom, eating a sandwich in the corridor on the way back? 'I was only a minute or so and didn't get a chance earlier,' was the reply! The supervision policy was written that night at home and delivered at the staff meeting the following day. And it was delivered not discussed. Sometimes, and only sometimes, dialogue did not happen: I told them. And this was one occasion.

I used to worry sometimes that some of them thought I was mad with the procedures we all went through. The irony was that the procedures were often needed with those who really should have known better. Sometimes that made me sad, but as time went on some of them began to catch on and, although nothing was said, they could see what was happening and why, and they began to trust me. I was consistent. I explained things and the reason was always the same – quality care and provision for the children.

I shared the beautiful story of Michelangelo chipping away at the marble block knowing that the masterful statue of David was inside, and how we, as teachers, should persist in attempting to reveal just a little more every day of the 'David' within every child. Perhaps on a wider scale, we as leaders do just the same with our staff. My staff could see where *we* were aiming for and they increasingly understood what the goals were. More importantly we were owning the goals, which were becoming alive and evident in the daily life of the school and were 'making a difference' to everyone.

I recall the following quote when reflecting back on this time: 'Vision is seeing the masterpiece while you are mixing the paints.'

I also recall feeling very isolated. The staff did not outwardly support me, but inwardly I knew they did. and at the time that was all I needed – it was enough to sustain me.

Communal codes (symbols and rituals)

One of the overwhelming issues that came up, when we had the initial pre-September chat, was behaviour. Most felt it was not bad but could be better – and they were right. There was a lack of consistently high expectation rife in school. There were very few agreed codes for the whole school. 'I don't think we are all doing the same thing,' said one teaching assistant vaguely to me one day. I nodded: this was the understatement of the year. So, we asked the children, all of them, what they wanted. They wanted rules. 'Why do we have to have rules?' I asked them. 'Because people will do as they are told then,' they said. 'Does it have to be that way?' I asked them? 'How about we have aims instead? Let's talk about how we want our school to be with just five statements and then let's think, with a sentence underneath, about how we can make that happen. What do we need to be doing to enable that to happen, what will it look like?' They *loved* it. And it worked, kept working and still is. They love the fact that they wrote the statements, they owned them and the teachers only helped and guided them. It worked a treat. Yes, we had sanctions but we rarely used them. It was simple and clear and we shared it with parents as well.

> 'It's like a second home here. We know where we are. We like the decorations and stuff on the walls as well and we are lucky.' (Emma, Year 4)

We did a similar exercise with our mission statement, as it was called then. We had some expert help to initiate the discussion, but it was written and owned by all. We took a day out and went away from school. We had a special lunch and a relaxed day with some quality input and we invited *everyone*. 'Gosh, we've never done this before – what a treat,' said one. Some did not come, even though the overtime was paid generously. 'This wasn't what I thought being a dinner lady was about', said one and so some of the casualties en route started as the school improvement train gained momentum and the balance tipped just a little. We were nowhere near the 'tipping point' but some stickiness had started. We had established our covenant of values. Now we had to live and breathe it.

Our codes and ways of being, started to develop further. We discussed what purposeful teaching environments looked like. We discussed what purposeful teaching looked like. Later, much later, we went on to look at what it *felt* like and how we could all link the learning triangle together but, for now, this was a huge step forward. We talked about our attitudes to people and our school, changes and challenges that we felt, and started to unpick what good-quality teaching and learning strategies were for us in our school, and how some of us had to adapt our practice to make sure it met the needs of our children and why we were doing it.

Developing our monitoring systems was hard. We really did have to 'face the brutal facts', as Jim Collins (2001) says. There was so much data around for our school that I *had* to share with them all that they had never seen. I wanted them to understand that we *had to* compare and challenge ourselves, we should have been consulting and competing with others, we had a moral obligation to be using all our resources to best effect and really adding value in *our* way to *our* children and other stakeholders.

Our partnerships were crucial for our organizational growth and they too had to see and understand what we were doing and why. We introduced simple home school agreements which were a synopsis of the mission statement and school code. We had 100 per cent sign up! Stakeholders felt involved and we were more consistent. Stakeholders felt valued and confident, and we gave them the time and information they wanted.

All of this was underpinned for me with one word: quality. Quality experiences for *all*. A quality environment for *all*. Quality resources for *all*. I had to lead by example: consistently and with high expectations of myself and those around me.

'You expect a lot but it will help us when we get to be *that* confident.'
(Sebastian, Year 3)

And it started in the first week when we all had to leave the hall and return ready and fit for purpose in every way – attitude, dress and demeanour – for the coming together time. We explained why to the children (and staff). In the early days I sometimes felt as if I was speaking a different language and it seemed so slow and painful at times. A funny ditty entitled 'Career advice 49' was sent to me on a postcard at the end of my first year. It said, 'Every good leader needs energy, wisdom and patience and occasionally a lie down.' The reservoir did need replenishing quite regularly. The five wells (emotional, physical, cognitive, spiritual and creative) that Jenny Mosley talks about were a huge part of my life (see www.circle-time.co.uk). I visited them quite regularly and of course relationships outside school were massively important.

Our 'assembling together' was a key feature and vehicle in establishing what ultimately became our collective identity. We met together regularly and at key times, with a common aim to renew, refresh and re-establish who we were and how we wanted to improve. We took small steps but they led to transformation ultimately. The structure of our week was very ritualistic with key times and key symbols to add clarity and purpose to what we were about.

The assembly cycle for the year was of a 'loose-tight' structure which enabled us to 'go with the flow' and allow the life of the school to take us to the next discussion (which it always did), as well as building in commitment to key festivals and times when we all knew what to expect.

'The Monday message and story gets me thinking what is coming up. If I'm not keen it gets me all fired up to give it a shot.' (Jordan, Year 6)

I remember one Candlemas celebration as we filled the hall with candles and calm, that the sense of warmth, (literally and otherwise!), love, togetherness and unspoken shared understanding was beyond belief.

'My spirit brightens up.' (Jamie, Year 4)

Music was a dimension that we all learned to understand the powerful significance of as well:

'We do understand what we are singing and even though you are still singing, it still gives you a message.' (Lucy, Year 3)

The staff – all of them – in turn, week by week, chose the music for the week and explained on Monday mornings why they had chosen it. It became OK to be vulnerable in our organization – or was it a becoming a community now? The adults began to share such personal and loving thoughts with us all about their music story, and we all valued, cherished and treasured that. And for me, time after time, after time, when I had chosen a theme for the week, it unknowingly matched with an aspect of the choice of music from a staff friend. I tingle once again as I reflect on the number of times that happened. Staff stopped asking me on Friday nights as they left if I had decided what the next theme of the week was going to be so that they could chose accordingly, because they trusted that all would align regardless on the Monday. We didn't just get a sense of community on those occasions, we felt the power globally!

Uniforms and identity were important as well. An outstanding member of my 'other' leadership team had the bright idea of extending our specific school uniform idea to the adults in school. We had a midday supervisor's uniform and a site manager's and cleaner's uniform, as well as one for the children. We had a board in school where we displayed the uniform and explained why we had one and why it was important to us. The uniform groups all had a token symbol attached to their group, with a challenge each week for the school community to work towards and attain. The sheer delight experienced every week, as the one school tie was awarded by peers to peers, or the dustpan and brush was displayed with pride in the cleanest classroom, or the lunchtime plaque and associated lunch box shelf stickers that went to a year group who had worked together, was evident time and time again.

And we had 'fuddles' as well. Another ritual that does, I believe, have some Eastern origin, which suggests that folk bring something and come together to eat, drink and talk. These became a regular feature at lunchtimes, particularly when we were celebrating or nearing the end of term, or sometimes just simply to bring us together. They were our version of the family meal.

We had established our codes and we all set off together. It was then that our behaviours began to change.

Dealing with the heat and resistance (leadership)

We talked and discussed a great deal *but* then we did action and stuck to it and sometimes I told them how it was going to be – nothing wrong with that in its time and place.

Display was a big one! No negotiation really, but plenty of explaining how and *why*! We went with a tight approach, originally, because I needed to get the point and impact across. We choose three colours for the displays and we all double mounted, using the same approach everywhere just for a term … and *wow*! Progression, continuity and real quality celebration of children's efforts! They got the hang of it quickly and then we all built on it from there. Some moaned and whinged a bit but then did do it and, I guess, sort of trusted, saw the point and then developed it themselves under steady eyes. Mind you, they also expected the same back from me and quite reasonably so.

They told me when it was all too much – 'We are going too fast Vanessa, could we slow down a bit please.' I hated cancelling those early November staff meetings – I had things planned and things we had to get on with but it would have been pointless to continue. They were asking for space and time and I had to keep them with me.

But we did hold the staff meetings later and we did keep the display policy up and running, and slowly the early delights and privileges of leading my new school began to emerge. We started to talk like a team; we started to act like a team. We knew all the team stuff going. We talked about bogs and islands, churches and hymn sheets, read Jim Collins' buses (that bit was not until much later) but it was starting to happen.

Our learning environment changed and adapted. We painted some things and threw other things out. Three professional development days were spent with skips for classrooms, cupboards and lofts, but why oh why did I then still see piles of 'but we just might need it' behind curtains and stock cupboards? We have all done it and continue to because we need security and, taking risks is fine when we know that the safety blanket is underneath … just in case.

And we kept on planning for the future. The authority and local builders gave us money for a new build. An extensive project started and we had two new classrooms and an office/admin/visitor area and new toilets and cloakrooms built.

It was so exciting and we then decorated and carpeted everywhere. What a feel-good factor! The place began to look alive and vibrant – fresh and fit for purpose. It became a place that people took a pride in and wanted to look good. The night before the Duke of York came to open the buildings, I had a little private wander round school after everyone had gone. The sense of pride and joy I felt was enormous and, if I am honest, it was really the first time I had felt that. I had waited two years for this feeling and tingle and here it was. Magical! The joy and recognition that the ship had turned, was pointing in the right direction and was gaining momentum was fantastic.

However, the other side of the coin was not quite as sunny. There were times when the reservoir felt near on empty, when I was faced with what appeared to be a paradoxical blend of personal humility and professional will.

Failing teachers and poor performance. How I hate even recalling those nights when I went home after yet another meeting with personnel and the unions, knowing we were one step further to firing the bullet, knowing that the last round of expensive focused support had not yet worked or been understood, also knowing that my colleague would be without a job and could not pay the mortgage if I pulled that trigger. Now here is where moral purpose and core values kick in – and hard. Of course I found it hard. Of course I struggled with what I was doing, but I never ever deep down questioned it. How can we question firing that bullet when your staff and children for year on year on year had not been getting what they were entitled to? Where does the 'they get one chance' argument fit in to that? So I did persevere and considered ultimatums as well. At one stage it was suggested that they could stay but accept demotion. Now my head really was on the parapet.

I had just got back from completing LPSH. I *knew* we were on the right lines and I knew that unless a certain member of staff went *completely* I could not do what I had set out, been appointed and was expected to do. So it was them or me – not an ultimatum just harsh reality.

She did move on under a glow of mystical cover about her future which nobody ever really did ask about. Even those who started, supported and encouraged the process with me found the last bit hard, and then one really is isolated apart from the faithful few. The legacy of underperformance is still evident today in school – and that hurts. They were lonely and isolated times. Staff members supported me discreetly and indirectly. Even when folk are with you they will not nail their flags to the mast, will they?

Would I do it all again? Yes, I would. How on earth can I not, I ask you? We have to embrace the sense of distinguishing role from self and lead with an open heart.

Actually, I did have to, on three more occasions but in different ways.

School improvement is about people, perspiration and process. Our staff and learners have a right to learn, to believe in themselves, and that is one of the privileges that we can make happen.

And then there was the opposite of that. I remember appointing one of my first newly qualified teachers (NQTs). He was quite something and was like a rocket in the staffroom. He painted his classroom yellow and turquoise and everyone gasped and could not believe I had let him. 'What were you thinking of?' they asked. 'Trusting him, giving him some autonomy, allowing him some space to create the learning environment that he had talked about so fantastically in his presentation, allowing him to model how I wanted it to be through out school when we were ready,' was my answer.

And slowly the team changed again and we developed into a full senior management team. We had a few hitches on the way though. We tried certain people in certain places and it lasted for a while and then was left but no harm done. What I did not do was put my strongest people on my greatest opportunities. I was still in the realms of strongest people on the greatest challenge. I would change that next time. The cycle had been started and when the time was right and the right people felt it was right, it did happen and within two years, by September 2003, we were really starting to pick up momentum.

Changing the environment and getting rid of millstones did make a huge difference. Fairness and justice are important. Folk were so much more receptive and willing that they were starting to actually believe in what we were doing and could see and feel the difference. Maybe we should push further?

And so we did.

The blossoming time (participation)

Real nitty-gritty stuff started in September 2003. There was a real energy about the place. We cranked it up again. We now had four of us leading – and we were leading. I say four, but actually the governing body was ready to fly further as well. We had an exceptional team with some very special people who gave and gave, and then went on to give a little bit more. I was truly blessed and our interdependence, both at individual level and community level, at that particular time was profound and, for me, unique. Our first external verification process was looming and we had to be ready and prepared.

All sounds good? It was but still I read the signs wrongly sometimes. I thought they were ready to talk the 'O' word (Ofsted). I got someone else in to gently start the process but I had not done my homework. I had not sussed out just how bad the last Ofsted inspection had been for them all. I had not asked them or discussed it. I had not sussed out why, had not sussed out what they were fearful of and I got a shock when I did. They had not been too worried last time as they knew *they* were basically OK and they knew that key issues of leadership and managements were not – the implication being that … they would be fairly left alone as the focus would be elsewhere. They did not tell me that of course – it came through my new leadership team investigating on our behalf. The staff were now going to team leaders instead of me. The trust was spreading and why? Well, team leaders had earned their stripes and were super role models and little sub-teams had been devised with clear expectations as to how they were going to operate. I had given them responsibility and with that, trust and respect, and so the model was extended.

I needed to move us forward again and include the 'O' word in our vocabulary and on our agenda, but for a while we just forgot about it. I did not actually forget it, but it felt like I had and it was just talked about at leadership team level. Then, very slowly, we talked about quality teaching and learning again – it improved some more – and we talked about subject leadership again and attempted to unpack all the potential worry bags that they had. So basically we talked and reassessed and tried to make sure that the team had what they needed, were not distracted and had some stability. It takes time – it does not happen overnight. Some of them willingly took on that challenge, embraced it and realized potential they never knew they had. Some of them had to be gently coerced and persuaded and I hear myself repeating the trust/value/invest words again. I guess nowadays you would call it workforce reform: removing all barriers. I wanted them to focus on what they were good at and without barriers.

I had once again learned through the process of me telling them and them telling me, and in time we did it together.

The early months of 2004, when we were inspected, were incredible – perhaps the most exciting time of all. It seemed as if it was the icing on the cake and everyone was on board. When the Ofsted inspection team did come I had but one objective – to get the due recognition that the school deserved for its hard work and commitment in recent years. I wanted the school community to have that external recognition that they now actually did believe of themselves. The team was good and thorough and many five-minute chats became over 40 minutes and, goodness, how defensive I became and fought my corner when I felt I was unfairly challenged – I am not sure where that passion came from.

The staff were amazing – only one small hiccup and the opening headlines of the report said:

> 'The school has made outstanding progress since the previous inspection. The school is now working effectively and improving still further. All the necessary steps have been taken for continuing improvement, and what is needed now is time for all the improvements to take full effect and raise the quality of provision and standards of attainment still further.'

We celebrated, the town community celebrated with us as well (it was important to them too) and we all went back through the headlines in the report and related them back to our original vision and ... they matched!

Even more amazing, as I evaluated my staff's opinions afterwards, was that they were tired but not fed up or demoralized. They were proud; they were looking forward (after a rest) to starting again and making it all even better. They *loved* the success and could see that it had all been worthwhile and they 'hadn't had anything to worry about really'.

And then we had a huge party and danced and celebrated and went away for the summer and that really was when I had some thinking to do – the 'original' vision had been achieved, where did we go next?

It was during this time that I really reflected on those around me to whom I referred to earlier as my other leadership team. I think most heads have a leadership team that includes the admin officers, the site manager and usually another one or two. After all, this study is about people and relationships and I have not talked specifically yet about the stories with Pam, Lucy, Suzanne and Brenda. Oh, and Mary, Jane, Paul and both Rebeccas. And how could the stories about Julia, Barbara, Amanda, Fiona and dear, dear Rachel at my right side, and, oh gosh, Keith and Yvonne, and those that came and went and those who would not go and those who are still there and … Mrs Hobson – say no more! And those new exciting roles we created – our learning mentors and inclusion managers, as we tried hard to find new ways to maintain our unswerving commitment to improving learning and achievement for those who were furthest behind. Do you need all of their stories? I think not. Perhaps better to reflect on how my interview questions and technique transformed over the six years, as those relationships changed me. So much so that somebody once said to me, 'You didn't ask much about the role, did you? Asked loads about me mind.'

I often reflect on that wonderful poem about how some people can come into your life for a reason or a season or a lifetime. Those that come for a reason are often short term. And those seasonal ones are often for a bit longer, as a phase is being gone through. I think I found some relationships of all types during that six years and am sure that some of them will be for a lifetime.

And after the blossoming (social networks)

So, what do you do when your goal has been reached? Do you think up another? Do you pack your bags? Do you have a rest? Nobody really tells you about that. Nobody tells you how it is post-Ofsted and post-accomplished goal. I guess if I had been an athlete I would have basked a little and then gone back into training and then looked ahead, with some guidance, at the next challenge and venue with a timescale. I guess, in a way, that is what I did.

It coincided with my being asked to extend the external work I was doing already and become a primary strategy consultant leader within the authority *and* be invited to join a leading-edge, pilot executive leadership programme with some of the best educationalists of our day. Quite frankly, the 12 days over that year inspired and enhanced my whole thinking about education across a social, political and economic spectrum. I really felt that I had had, as the Hebrew word *ruah* expresses so beautifully, new life breathed into me.

I began to think in a less tangible outcomes driven way and started writing the 'how do I want it to feel' list rather than the 'how do I want it to look' list which had been the necessary way previously. So, with secure roots and solid foundations now in place, I really wanted us to think about being a premier school. Continuing to cultivate those now strong relationships was of paramount importance. I wanted to balance the developing culture and ethos in the school with tradition and innovation, but above all maximize that positive energy that was now flowing throughout school so that we could really become a learning community. We had our team and teams now, and they were empowered and enabled. They were also valued and valuable and they knew it.

This was an in between time and in some ways very exciting – probably a time when a great deal was happening but I did not realize. I networked beyond just the region now and others on the staff started to do the same. I visited a school overseas and became involved in some initiatives nationally that all influenced us. We sifted through the pile and chose what was appropriate and we really began to sail beyond the horizon. We continued with some tangible ideas in school at the time. We worked on the curriculum and continuing professional development (CPD) took another huge step forward. Parental involvement took on a new look and we really engaged with thinking skills and learning styles across the whole school.

I read a great deal as well – it is so important to read and intellectualize what we do as well as getting out there and doing it – and I took many articles to the leadership team and key governors. Were we capable of moving from good to great? Were we capable of looking in the mirror and out of the window as part of our self-evaluation processes? Could we start to look at those characteristics that level five leaders have? Could I break those levels down further and start enabling those skills to be developed from NQT level? Were we capable of now moving from the micro to the macro, from our institution to the system? We had to continue to build the capacity for change and sustained improvement? We had the freedom and we had the choice but I also had to ensure with the team that we still kept the accountability and rigour there. It felt strange because this time, although we were clear about the defined end game, the means were not that clear – at least not for a while.

And of course we had to keep focused on the reason as to why we were there! I think *my* biggest challenge was to ascertain and be clear as to whether I had gained sufficient entry with the school community to be able to move us all on again. Sounds, from the story, as if I had succeeded. But as leaders we still continue to not always read the situation appropriately and, of course, sometimes the playing fields and the players change and then one really does look to see how strong those walls are and whether the ether really does seep through and beyond like a seamless thread.

Csikszentmihalyi (1997) talks so beautifully about flow – the ultimate synergy of high challenge and high skill. During the next year or so, I experienced some real flow but also had some brutal facts to confront, yet I still had to remain optimistic. I wanted something for the school, which it had never had, and sometimes when one is in that situation you have to do what you have never done.

The second vision (interdependence and reciprocity)

I went back to the governors and staff (and children in a way) with a second vision – the learning-centred school.

School culture and climate with a high priority focus on learning. School leadership, particularly middle leadership, and developing teachers and students as learners!

We were deemed highly effective by the local authority that year and we received Investor in People (IiP) which really did touch on, in the report, the strength of our relationships, climate and our moral purpose, in fact our moral excellence!

One of the delights of this second vision was how it was no longer a concrete tangible and structured programme. Rather it was an organic process. The shift from an improvement top-down approach to self-evaluation from within, from attainment to achievement, from teaching to learning and from management to leadership, were all so apparent with the new message for the next system-led phase from the community we had become.

We all engaged in conversation and debate again. 'The simplest and most powerful investment any member of a community can make in *renewal* is to begin talking with other people as if the answers mattered.'

We had relational trust in the team; there was respect and regard for each other and we had integrity and it was actually the children at this point who were truly amazing in taking hold of the new vision.

We spent a month in a variety of ritual 'coming togethers' as classes or year groups or whole school to articulate and define what the ideal learner, as adult or child, should look like and feel like – metaphorically you understand, although one little star did say that he thought someone like that should be wearing glasses!

> 'I think the ideal learner should always think before you react and say something. But sometimes it does still pop out of your mouth.' (Harry, Year 2)

They told me what the lead learner should be like as well! Gosh, some little improvements there for me to think about too! We unpicked our learning environments again. We asked ourselves what we wanted the ideal place for learning to look and feel like, and then we went about making it happen. We called it our learning triangle – our job descriptions – and that for the triangle to stay together in that structure we had to ensure all three sides stuck together at the corners.

We recalled the 'highly effective' status that we had received from the local authority and we all looked at the criteria together and articulated what exactly it was that we did to make us highly effective and why. And don't children tell you exactly how it is!

'I'm sure it has something to do with people.' (Sam, Year 1)

'We join in and we try to make sure everyone is included.' (Ella, Year 1)

Some of the occasions I have listed here were truly my most transcendent and spiritual; where the senses of compassion and caring, engagement and commitment were at their peak. The community had found real deep meaning; they were confident and valued their contributions and those of others.

'Sometimes I think we take it for granted but when it's lost it's gone. I've learnt more now about how to appreciate. It makes me feel warm and bubbly.' (Catherine and Katie, Year 5)

We were securely aligned. We were authentic. We had transformed.

I think ultimately that while we did have ambition, clarity and focus, we also needed to have timing and emotional intelligence and an awareness of dragons around the corner. Of course, the challenge and real skill is to manage all those together, to be secure that all members of the community were still engaged and committed. And I could not start the process this time by myself, as that was no longer appropriate. Even if I had a definite sense of purpose, firm convictions and was steady with the unique style and substance that we had all been familiar with in the past, this time was different.

Staff were supportive and 'up for it', governors were not as keen. Perhaps I should have thought longer and more sensitively about the situation. New, eager but inexperienced faces and a new team that had not had time to gel yet and a change in key players – my chair and vice-chair and a few key chairs of committees – *and* dragons around the corner. Maybe at a time when the human face of school change was at its most fragile in one area, my model of professional entrepreneurialship was not wholly appropriate. We had worked hard at this in the past, extending my style and experience through the team that enabled some staff members to have a whole new chapter to explore. But this time we were getting stuck as we tried to work our way through new levels and types of trust.

We worked hard, I worked hard to share the message and the value of it to the new governing team, but these were indeed rocky times with some hard questions to ask of myself and those around me. I had experienced a step change. The landscape around me had changed and so, therefore, had my mindscape.

But what about those around me? Could they, did they want to make the step change as well, or had we made enough strides already? Those key characteristics of a community with high social capital were no longer there sufficiently enough with my governors in May 2005. Our original shared social norms and values were shaky and we had not been able to maintain that interdependence and reciprocity. That original bonding had become unstuck. We had lost the strong sense of alignment and, dare I say it, brotherhood? We were shaky in that inspiring art form, 'boundaryless possibility thinking' as Benjamin Zander (Zander and Zander, 2002) suggests.

I wonder if I should have read *Leading Minds* by Gardner again at the time. He talks about instinct and intuition, a sense of timing – the ability to stand back and reflect and learn. I think I did have the ability to see and keep the big picture in mind and I was resilient and willing to take risks and ready to confront authority, but let us go back to the instinct and intuition. I think, actually, it was there and strong and I chose to 'meddle'.

The parting of company (social capital)

We did work well for a good year after the new vision was finally agreed and accepted, with some scepticism from a few, but I certainly felt that the road was now a potential slope and it did feel slippery at times. I felt that we were in danger of 'having had the experience but missing the meaning' in the words of T. S. Eliot.

I decided to part company with our community creation a year later and it was the right thing to do for everyone. I asked my Year 6 learners during their exit interviews, to say the first word that came into their heads when I said our school name. Following is the top ten:

- calm
- magical
- inclusive
- amazing
- secret
- welcome
- bright
- learn
- happy
- love.

It was one of the hardest things I have ever done – I recalled General George S. Patton Jr's words as I sat in the governors' meeting announcing my resignation – 'today you must do more than is required of you. Never think that you have done enough or that your job is finished' (www.generalpatton.com/quotes). It was appropriate and right. I think a good leader should always know and act upon the feeling of knowing when their time is up and be ready emotionally to implement that when you share the news with others so that you can still lead them through the transition.

No regrets at all, but a natural curiosity as to how the future will evolve for the community as once again it enters a culture of change. Just what are those walls made of now and what do they contain? Are they strong and uniquely distinctive or are they quietly trembling at the irrational fear of the unknown? Will that spiritual ether continue to wind its way like a seamless thread? Does the moral code belong to the very being of the community now in its own right?

> 'Even though you think you have seen it once you can still never explain it but you know it is there. You can try to speak it but it's your mind that knows. Like a secret really.' (Emily, Year 6)

As I said my final goodbye, the place still felt warm and giving, secure and forgiving. But it was also ready and prepared for the next phase – strong enough now to stand alone and upright. Ready to flourish and blossom as the older fruit drops away and the new buds start to emerge; ready to be a community where people discover their talents rather than a school where children are educated.

> 'It feels right here. The school is the heart isn't it? I always think that even when it is grey outside, it is summer inside.' (Lily, Year 6)

References

Aldgate, J., Jones, D., Rose, W. and Jeffery, C. (eds) (2006) *The Developing World of the Child*, London: Jessica Kingsley Publishers

Archard, D. (2004) *Children Rights and Childhood 2nd Edition*, Abingdon: Routledge

Armstrong, J. (2004) *The Secret Power of Beauty*, London: Penguin

Barber, M. (1997) *The Learning Game*, London: Indigo

Battle, M. (1997) *Reconciliation*, Cleveland, Ohio: The Pilgrim Press

Bolman, L. G. and Deal, T. E. (1995) *Leading with Soul*, San Francisco, Calif.: Jossey-Bass Inc.

Brandt, R. (1998) *Powerful Learning*, Alexandria, Virg.: Association for Supervision and Curriculum Development (ASCD)

Burke, C. and Grosvenor, I. (2003) *The School I'd Like*, Abingdon: RoutledgeFalmer

Bryk, A. S. and Schneider, B. (2002) *Trust in Schools*, New York: Russell Sage Foundation

Capra, F. (1996) *The Web of Life*, London: HarperCollinsPublishers

Capra, F. (2002) *The Hidden Connections,* London: HarperCollinsPublishers

Catterall, A. (2007) *The Guardian Guide*, 5–11 May, London: The Guide

Clements, A. and Aung S. S. K. (1997) *The Voice of Hope*, London: Penguin Books

Collins, J. (2001) *Good to Great,* New York: HarperCollins

Comte-Sponville, A. (1996) *A Short Treatise on the Great Virtues*, London: William Heinemann

Craft, A. (2002) *Creativity and Early Years Education*, London: Continuum

Csikszentmihalyi, M. (1997) *Finding Flow,* New York: Basic Books

Cunningham. M. (2006) *The Invention of Childhood*, London: BBC Books

Dawkins, R. (2006) *The God Delusion*, London: Bantam Press

Dewey, J. (1933) *How We Think*, Boston Mass.: Houghton Mifflin Company

Diamond, J. (2005) *Collapse*, London: Penguin Allen Lane

Etzioni, A. (1995) *The Spirit of Community*, London: Fontana Press

Flutter, J. and Rudduck, J. (2004) *Consulting Pupils What's in it for Schools?*, London: RoutledgeFalmer

Fullan, M. (2001) *Leading in a Culture of Change*, San Francisco, Calif.: Jossey-Bass

Gardner, H. (1995) *Leading Minds, An Anatomy of Leadership,* New York: Basic Books

Gardner, H. (1999) *The Disciplined Mind*, New York: Simon & Schuster

Gardner, H. (2006a) *The Development and Education of the Mind*, Abingdon: Routledge

Gardner, H. (2006b) *Five Minds for the Future*, Boston, Mass.: Harvard Business School Publishing

Gibbs, J. M. (2007) 'Justice is better than vengeance', the *Independent*,12 April, Education pages 6–7

Glazer, S. (ed.) (1999) *The Heart of Learning*, New York: Tarcher/Putnam

Goldberg, E. (2005) *The Wisdom Paradox*, New York: Gotham Books

Goleman, D. (1996) *Emotional Intelligence*, London: Bloomsbury Publishing

Goleman, D. (2006) *Social Intelligence*, London: Hutchinson

Grahame, K. (1994) *Wind in the Willows*, London: HarperCollinsPublishers

Grayling, A. C. (2001) *The Meaning of Things*, London: Weidenfeld & Nicolson

Grayling, A. C. (2002) *The Reason of Things*, London: Weidenfeld & Nicolson

Guignon, C. (2004) *On Being Authentic*, London: Routledge

Hargreaves, D. and Fink, D. (2006) *Sustainable Leadership*, San Francisco, Calif.: Jossey-Bass

Havel, V. (1990) *Disturbing the Peace*, London: Faber & Faber

Hay, D. with Nye, R. (1998) *The Spirit of the Child*, London: Fount Paperbacks

Hayward, J. and Jones, G. (2001) 'Activities speak louder than words', *Teaching Thinking*, Summer (4), pages 16–20

Heaney, S. (1996) *Death of a Naturalist*, London: Faber and Faber

Hick, J. (1999) *The Fifth Dimension*, Oxford: Oneworld Publications

Holloway, R. (2004) *Godless Morality*, Edinburgh: Canongate Books

Kessler, R. (2000) *The Soul of Education: Helping students find connection, compassion, and character in school*, Alexandria, Virg.: Association for Supervision and Curriculum Development (ASCD)

Kübler-Ross, E. and Kessler, D. (2005) *On Grief and Grieving*, London: Simon & Schuster UK

Dalai Lama, 'Education and the human heart', in Glazer, S. (ed.) (1999) *The Heart of Learning*, New York: Tarcher/Putnam

Law, S. (2006) *The War for Children's Minds*, London: Routledge

Layard, R. (2005) *Happiness*, London: Allen Lane

Leithwood, K., McAdie, P., Bascia, N. and Rodrigue, A. (2006) *Teaching for Deep Understanding*, Thousand Oaks, Calif.: Corwin Press

Lickona, T. (1992) *Educating for Character*, New York: Bantam Books

Maathai, W. M. (2007) *Unbowed*, London: William Heinemann

MacIntyre, A. (1966) *A Short History of Ethics*, New York: Macmillan

Martin, J. (2006) *The Meaning of the 21st Century*, London: Eden Project Books

Martin, P. (2005) *Making Happy People*, London: Fourth Estate

Mason, M. and Dearden, J. (2004) *Snapshots of Possibility*, London: The Alliance for Inclusive Education

Matthews, G. B. (1994) *The Philosophy of Childhood*, Cambridge, Mass.: Harvard University Press

McIntosh, A. (2004) *Soil and Soul*, London: Aurum Press

Moxley, R. S. (2000) *Leadership Spirit*, San Francisco, Calif.: Jossey-Bass

National Playing Fields Association (2000) *Best Play: what play provision should do for children*, London: National Playing Fields Association

O'Donohue, J. (1997) *Anam Cara*, London: Bantam Books Edition

O'Hara, K. (2004) *Trust From Socrates to Spin*, London: Icon Books

O'Leary, D. J. (2001) *Travelling Light*, Blackrock, Dublin: The Columba Press

O'Sullivan, E. (1999) *Transformative Learning*, Toronto: University of Toronto Press

Palmer, S. (2006) *Toxic Childhood*, London: Orion Books

Perkins, D. (1998) *Smart Schools*, New York: Simon & Schuster

Pritchard, M. S. (1996) *Reasonable Children*, Lawrence, Kansas: University Press of Kansas

Putnam, R. D. (2000) *Bowling Alone*, New York: Simon & Schuster

QCA (1999) *National Curriculum on line: PSHE*, London: QCA, available online at: www.nc.uk.net

Richardson, P. T. (1996) *Four Spiritualities*, Palo Alto, Calif.: Davies-Black Publishing

Sacks, J. (2000) *The Politics of Hope*, London: Vintage

Senge, P. M. (1990) *The Fifth Discipline*, New York: Doubleday Currency

Sergiovanni, T. J. (1992) *Moral Leadership*, San Francisco, Calif.: Jossey-Bass

Sergiovanni, T. J. (1995) *The Principalship: a reflective practice perspective 3rd Edition*, Needham Heights, Mass.: Allyn and Bacon

Singer, P. (1997) *How are we to live?* Oxford: Oxford University Press

Sizer, T. R. and Sizer, N. F. (1999) *The Students are Watching*, Boston, Mass.: Beacon Press

Spivey, N. (2005) *How Art Made the World*, London: BBC Books

Steiner, G. (2003) *Lessons of the Masters*, Cambridge, Mass.: Harvard University Press

Tacey, D. (2003) *The Spirituality Revolution*, Sydney: HarperCollins

Taylor, C. (1989) *Sources of the Self*, Cambridge: Cambridge University Press

Taylor, C. (1991) *The Ethics of Authenticity*, Cambridge, Mass.: Harvard University Press

Taylor, H. and Pite, V. (2006) *Leading the Way*, *Improvement*, Winter, pages 13–16

UNICEF (2007) Report Card 7 *Child poverty in Perspective: An overview of child well-being in rich countries*, Florence, Italy: UNICEF Innocenti Research Centre

Vernon, M. (2005) *The Philosophy of Friendship*, Basingstoke: Palgrave Macmillian

West-Burnham, J. and Coates, M. (2005) *Personalizing Learning: transforming education for every child*, Stafford: NetworkEducational Press

West-Burnham, J., Farrar, M. and Otero, G. (2007) *Schools and Communities: working together to transform children's lives*. London: Network Continuum Education

White, L. (2000) *Reflection Time*, London: National Society/Church House Publishing

Wittgenstein, L. (1958) *Philosophical Investigations*, London: Blackwell

Zander, R. and Zander, B. (2002) *The Art of Possibility*, Cambridge, Mass.: Harvard Business School Press

Zeldin, T. (1998) *Conversation*, London: The Harvill Press

Zohar, D. and Marshall, I. (2000) *Spiritual Intelligence The Ultimate Intelligence*, London: Bloomsbury Publishing

Index

Also available from Network Continuum

Schools and Communities – John West-Burnham, Maggie Farrar and George Otero

Personalizing Learning – John West-Burnham and Max Coates

Promoting Children's Well-Being in the Primary Years – ed. Andrew Burrell and Jenii Riley

Inspirations – Tim Woodhouse and David Woods

Becoming Emotionally Intelligent – Catherine Corrie

Toon Cards – Chris Terrell

Self Intelligence – Steve Bowkett

Inclusion in Schools: Making a Difference – Rosemary Sage

Leading Change in Schools – Sian Case